LISTEN VERY CAREFULLY, I SHALL SAY THIS ONLY ONCE

LISTEN VERY CAREFULLY, I SHALL SAY THIS ONLY ONCE

An autobiography

JEREMY LLOYD

BBC BOOKS

Picture Credits

BBC Books would like to thank the following for providing photographs
and for permission to reproduce copyright material. While every effort has
been made to trace and acknowledge all copyright holders, we would like
to apologise should there have been any errors or omissions.

Numbers refer to plate pages.

(c) BBC: 7, 8 (above); Alan Davidson Photography: 8 (below); Ronald
Grant Archive: 1 (below right); Hulton Deutsch Collection: 6 (below left
and right); Angus McBean: 5 (below); Movie Acquisitions UK/British
Film Institute: 2 (above) and 3 (below); Paramount Pictures/British Film
Institute: 5 (above); Rank Organization/British Film Institute: 3 (above),
6 (above). Other pictures courtesy of the author.

Published by BBC Books,
a division of BBC Enterprises Limited,
Woodlands, 80 Wood Lane, London W12 0TT

First published 1993
© Jeremy Lloyd 1993
ISBN 0 563 36203 0

Set in Calisto by Selwood Systems, Midsomer Norton
Printed and bound in Great Britain by Butler & Tanner Ltd,
Frome and London
Jacket printed by Lawrence Allen Ltd, Weston-super-Mare

CONTENTS

Chapter One   1

Chapter Two   22

Chapter Three   30

Chapter Four   44

Chapter Five   67

Chapter Six   87

Chapter Seven   104

Chapter Eight   121

Chapter Nine   132

Chapter Ten   150

Index   168

For my dear friend,

Johnny Gold,

for a thousand chats.

he happens to read this book. Our partnership started in about 1970, when I dropped him a line suggesting a show about a department store. His wife Ann cooked such a good lunch, that I was relieved to find he *was* keen on the idea, which resulted in more splendid lunches as we ate and laughed our way through sixty-nine episodes of *Are You Being Served?*, based loosely on my life as a junior slave in the Gents Natty Suiting Department at Simpson of Piccadilly.

Recently on a trip to Miami, I sat in a Holiday Inn watching an endless succession of *Are You Being Served?* from the early seventies and I was surprised that I could remember half the jokes before they actually arrived. But then in the writing world it's common knowledge that there are only seven original jokes. So we've clearly managed to recycle them around the world quite a few times, despite a few punctures and tyre changes.

I might never have been fortunate enough to become a writer, had I not been lucky enough to be such a failure at everything else. The great thing about failure is it provides many different walks of life to fail in. I can say with some pride, that at school I was a complete all rounder in the failure stakes and I'm sorry not to have kept my reports to prove it.

My first failure was to be a child that was not wanted by my father or mother as they had parted shortly after I was born. My father apparently ran off with the girl-next-door. There might have been somebody more suitable further down the street, but I understand he was always impetuous when young.

It was decided that I should be put into the care of my grandparents who lived in Didsbury, a suburb of Manchester. I think I was about one year old when I was taken to the station in London where my grandmother took me from my mother and promised to look after me. In later years my mother complained that I never even looked back or waved as I boarded the train. As it was the first train I'd seen, I'm not surprised. Trains were a very exciting experience.

My grandmother, on my father's side, was a very motherly woman, much liked by everybody, and I took to her immediately. I was taken home to meet my grandfather. They had a nice flat at Number One, Winster Avenue, off the Barlomoor Road. Downstairs there were two aunts, Sissy and Flossy. I don't think they were really aunts, but I was always told they were my aunts.

Life in the early thirties in Didsbury was fairly uneventful. The main excitement was being able to cycle round the garden on my three-wheeler and play with Oswald my tortoise. My grandmother got very bored reading to me and made sure that I was able to read for myself. By the time I was three, I seemed to do nothing but read comics and play with toy soldiers. Oswald always played a tank and by sticking plasticine on his back, I was able to make him carry a great number of toy soldiers about. I think he really enjoyed it. I was always being given things to build me up, such as Virol, a ghastly sticky treacly preparation. And if I had a sore throat my grandmother would bake a potato, put it in a stocking and wrap it round my neck. I can't think why, because I'm sure cough mixture must have been invented by then. The big excitement in the afternoon was to listen to *Children's Hour*: Larry the Lamb, Mr Grouser and Dennis the Dachshund were great favourites. I really thought they existed. Such was the power of radio.

We also had a maid in those days called Chrissie: a very thin Irish woman, with fingers stained brown from smoking Piccadilly cigarettes, which she used to buy in packets of five. The first job I had was going to the shops to buy cigarettes for her. I was probably only five at the time, but little boys could walk half a mile without fear of being molested in those days. There was of course the constant threat hanging over me that I was nearly old enough to go to school. I'd had very little contact with children and wasn't looking forward to it at all; I cried a lot as I was taken to the South Manchester Junior Grammar School in Didsbury Village and introduced to Miss Hardisty, who taught the Juniors. To my surprise it turned out to be great fun; I'd sit there chanting my twelve times table with the rest of them, then hurry to plasticine class, then out to the playgound to race our dinky toys, and then back to make paper villages and learn copper-plate handwriting.

After two years I was very good at handwriting and plasticine and had made quite a few friends, who were sometimes allowed to come to our house for tea, so we could all listen to *Children's Hour* together on the radio. Then the radio took on a more sinister tone; my grandfather spent every evening twiddling with the knobs, listening to news bulletins. I was aware that something serious was happening in the world. The invasion of Poland was often mentioned and Hitler. But it never really came home to us, until the day we sat round the radio listening to the announcer say that we were at war with Germany. My only experience with Germany up to that date had been that they made great caps for my toy pistol and that I had a Schuco car with gears and remote controls, all stamped 'Made in Germany'. Suddenly we had gas mask practice at school; most of us cried when we put them on. Then the barrage balloons started to go up.

My grandparents decided it was too dangerous for me to remain in Didsbury and I was shipped off to boarding school in Cheshire. I remember my grandfather's Rover entering the gates of a rather forbidding looking establishment with grey walls where I met for the first time the demon Doctor Dunwell, the dog-collared headmaster of this private Colditz. He was a very hairy man. He had hair everywhere: the back of his hands, out of his ears, even out of his nose. I'd never seen so much hair. He was very charming on our first meeting.

'Does the boy play football?'

'Oh yes,' said Grandma, 'he loves it.'

'Does he kick with the toe or the instep?' He looked at me quizzically.

'My toe,' I said.

'We'll soon cure that,' said Doctor Dunwell. 'Will he be taking shooting?'

I nodded vigorously.

'He's made a bow and arrow,' said my grandmother. 'He's very keen.'

'Piano lessons?'

My grandfather shook his head. 'Definitely not.'

This was one of the few times I heard my grandfather speak; he was a very silent man, who had a silent whistle, and had I been a bat I would probably have been able to communicate with him better. I tried not to cry as the Rover drove out through the gates to disappear back towards warm, comfortable Didsbury. I was given cocoa and biscuits and introduced to the boys. Doctor Dunwell's charm disappeared as swiftly as my grandparents' car. And I knew I wasn't going to enjoy myself. I was right. After my cocoa and biscuits Doctor Dunwell invited me to his study to assess my knowledge; I apparently fell far short of the requirements of Harden House. And he remarked on more than one occasion that trying to teach me was like trying to hang a hat on a missing peg. This needless to say was the outer limit of Doctor Dunwell's humour.

Strangely enough, for a man of the cloth, he was unsparingly energetic in his attempts to beat knowledge into us: staring grimly through his rimless spectacles as he beat us in his study during the day. Then to add a High Church note to the proceedings he'd don his purple silk dressing gown at night and creep about the corridors until he imagined he'd heard somebody whispering in one of the dormitories. It took a great effort of will not to die of fright when he appeared, cane at the ready, a purple vision of corrective punishment. He spoke, in a deep vibrant voice: 'Hands up, the boys who were talking? No one. I see. In that case I shall beat you all!' This was one of the rare times he smiled. Doctor Dunwell is probably the main reason I've never attended a tarts and vicars party.

I shall always remember my first night in that dormitory; having suffered the indignity of being nicknamed 'Beaky' because of a long nose, I had to undergo the rigorous test that all new boys had to undergo: that is to climb out of the window, crawl along the ledge and reappear at the other window. As it was quite a long drop to the ground, this was rather exciting. Particularly as the other window was shut, just as I got to it, as was the custom. I had to plead for it to be opened. Then a dash across everybody's bed, being hit by wet-knotted towels, a scramble on hands and knees, trying to protect myself and back to bed. I hadn't cried, so I was considered all right. I was quite lucky really. When engaged in such a similar initiation test a year later, I remember a new boy slipping and banging his head on the sharp corner of the mantelpiece. His cries were muffled with a pillow, as we examined the damage. Somebody swore they could see a grey tube sticking out. It was assessed to be part of his brain that had popped out from behind the ear. We stuck a plaster on it and told him not to mention this to anybody. Needless to say, he never did well at lessons. But then neither did I.

One of the boys, known as 'The Pig', lost an eye during the holidays on a rambling excursion and appeared at school with a glass one, which gave him rather a fixed stare. He didn't seem particularly concerned about losing his eye and would often take the glass one out at breakfast just to put us off our toast. He seemed positively to enjoy receiving so much horrified attention, until one night in the dormitory he took it out to play marbles. Somebody jumped on it for a joke. So he had to wear a patch after that, as his family refused to buy him a new one.

I must say boarding school days were quite the unhappiest ones of my life. Doctor Dunwell cut costs wherever he could. There were two wooden outside classrooms, which in the winter were completely unheated, except for a small stove, with doors that you could close. The fire was not lit until about fifteen minutes before we'd arrive at the classroom. The ink wells were quite often frozen over. And in the few minutes we had waiting for a teacher to appear, small boys were picked on by the larger ones, and roasted in front of the fire. Come to think of it, it wasn't so much a school as a training ground for terrorists.

The usual subjects – history, maths, Latin, geography, at which I was appalling, and religion, at which I was jolly good – were all taught, although not often imprinted on the conscious mind. I remember struggling with Latin and wondering how often I'd be able to have a conversation in this archaic language with other people when I left school. So far – none. Though I suppose it would be useful in Italian restaurants, but there is usually a translation on the menu.

As far as menus went at school, it seemed to be a foot-high pile of toast between each table for breakfast with an inevitable pot of Silver Shred marmalade. Every boy had his own pot. The exciting breakfast game would be to turn the pots upside down and see whose bubble rose to the end of the jar first. Lunch was meat and two veg, followed by rice pudding or Spotted Dick, then cocoa and biscuits around six, and as far as I can recall, nothing else at all. Which meant we all had to rely on out tuck boxes that our families were supposed to send us to supplement our diet. The small boys had their tuck boxes taken immediately and the contents were handed out amongst the older ones. This booty was then hidden beneath the floorboards and finding a half-nibbled bag of crisps and a sausage roll that would retreat, as you reached for it, was more exciting to think about than actually participate in. Boarding school life was really the survival of the fittest, or the most mentally deranged.

We had a very tall teacher who was fondly referred to as 'Uncle'. I don't know why. He became deranged one night when a new boy had to undergo the assault course and initiation. The boy had leapt off the bed and grabbed the overhead light to escape the attentions of his new chums. The bulb and socket came away in his hands and he landed with a loud cry, attracting the attention of the aforesaid 'Uncle'. The light had been switched on while this occurred, so the ends of the wires were now bare and hanging from the ceiling. 'Uncle' was tall enough to connect with them in the dark and lit up with a bright flash. He collapsed, his pipe still clamped in his teeth. We shone a torch on him.

'Cripes,' said someone, 'he's definitely dead.'

'We'll say we didn't do it,' said somebody else.

Such excuses were to no avail, we all received a severe thrashing from the cane happy Doctor Dunwell. 'Uncle' had quite a spring in his step for quite a long time after.

The only useful thing we learnt was how to make gun powder. Unfortunately, we could never make quite enough to blow up the school. During these formative years my first writing efforts showed a brief glimmer: a hero in one of our favourite comics, either *Hotspur* or *The Wizard* decided to kill off Red Mask, a daredevil flyer from World War One. I had enjoyed Red Mask, and with scratchy pen and questionable spelling, I continued his adventures in my exercise book for a further three weeks, reading it to the class before lessons. The demon Doctor Dunwell listened to episode three through the keyhole and I spent the rest of the week standing up for the misuse of an exercise book!

As the reader will gather school days got the adrenal glands up to full steam in double quick time. Underweight and puny, with large spectacles and one lens blacked out to improve the sight of a dodgy eye, I became a brilliant runner. At the first hint of bullying I was off like a rocket, not always successfully. I do remember blubbering, in a neck-lock as my pet caterpillar was beheaded in front of me. We were learning about the French Revolution at the time and Madame Guillotine had made a deep impression on us. I've never kept in touch with anyone from school. I wonder why?

On the plus side, I have fond memories of flying model aeroplanes on a warm summer's evening in the playing field. They were mainly Spitfires and Hurricanes made by a firm called Frog (For rising off ground). And to see those flying high above our heads, then landing on the cricket pitch was a moment of great excitement. In fact, I feel like flying one now, except the patio is a bit small.

How different those days were from school life as portrayed today. Sex was never discussed. The main interest being boyish pursuits, such as boxing, football and beating up small boys. And of course being conversant with popular expressions such as 'Wizard prang'; 'Good show'; 'Pax'; 'Cavee' and 'Cripes'. In fact, the only time that sex was seriously discussed was when the Matron's bathroom plumbing went awry. She announced she would be conducting her ablutions in our dormitory bath-room; this was separated from the dormitory by a stout door. The news caused great excitement and a serious discussion took place as to whether we'd be able to see her in the altogether through the key hole. It was decided that the chance of a brief glimpse seemed to be remote. For a guaranteed first-time look at the female body, it was necessary to place a mirror at a strategic angle on the wash basin, which when viewed through the key hole would reflect whatever appeared in the bath. This was not a suggestion of mine, but that of a Greek, by the name of Thomieades, who was always tops at maths. Breathlessly, we queued up as the water plunged from the ancient taps and thundered into the large metal bath. Smallest boys at the rear, boys with the largest pimples at the front. I removed the detach-able eye patch from my glasses and waited for my turn.

Matron was known to the boys as 'The Hairpin'. This was due to her slim build, she was probably in her late twenties, but to us, she seemed to be in the full bloom of autumn. Finally the water stopped. By then some boys at the front had been holding their breath so long that they had already collapsed, so the queue got shorter and I found myself near the front. Through the faint light in the dormitory window I could see that the first boy was visibly moved by what he had seen. The second stayed so long that I was afraid 'The Hairpin' might get out before it was my turn. Finally, I bent down and looked through the key hole. The mirror had steamed up, I could see nothing. We questioned the two who had seen something.

From their description, it was decided that chums were infinitely preferable to girlfriends. And it was clear that athletic sports were adequate compensation compared with the trivial pursuit of the opposite sex. Having reached this momentous turning point in our lives, we retired to bed, and took up our positions in the Flying Fortress. This was an imaginary plane our dormitory flew at night to bomb Berlin. The small boys were made to keep the drone of the engines going, while the more intelligent pinched their noses between thumb and forefinger and had nasal conversations which took place between rear-gunner, pilot, co-pilot and navigator. There were frequent warnings from the gun turrets of 'Look out ME109 on Port Wing'; or 'This is the pilot. Bombs gone'; or from the co-pilot, 'Wizard prang'; and 'Cripes, this is the radio operator, my legs have been blown off'. To which the pilot would reply, 'Bad luck, sparks, hang in there.' This desperate battle against overwhelming odds resulted in a bid to get home on two engines. Not surprisingly Doctor Dunwell appeared just as we had reached Dover, resplendent in his purple dressing gown and bending a favourite cane. He mercilessly beat the pilot, co-pilot, navigator, rear-gunner and the now dead wireless operator – the loss of his legs proving fatal. Then Doctor Dunwell turned his attention to the engine noises, before retiring with a satisfied smile. I think the only round we ever won against him was to be able to imitate an air raid siren so realistically that the panic-stricken Doctor, aided by 'The Hairpin', shepherded us down to the cellars, fearful that Cheshire was about to receive its first air raid. Unfortunately, it was unheated. We froze to death until morning, at which time, of course, there had still been no 'all clear'. It was decided by unanimous vote not to repeat this experience.

We all looked forward with desperation to school holidays. If the waiting became too much, we would try to invent illnesses which would result in us being taken home. I complained of an imaginary stomachache and got to the point when an ambulance was about to be sent for. It was only the words, 'we may have to operate immediately', that convinced me I should make a miraculous recovery which I did. When I did get home, I had very little communication with Grandpa Sydney who was an inventor and worked for the Metropolitan Vicker's Engineering Company, and was obviously so intelligent that conversations with small boys were out of the question. He would often look at me quizzically whilst polishing his pipe on the side of his nose. I think he felt I was rather an intruder in the family, which indeed I was.

During these past few years I had seen very little of my mother. Perhaps no more than two or three times when she had come to visit. This was probably due to the fact that she was in show business. She was a very pretty woman with blonde hair, very blue eyes, and perfect teeth. In fact, she was so pretty that she advertised Craven A Cigarettes. I believe it was one of their first campaigns. Her poster was often on buses, and Gran would always point her out as she passed by. In fact, I saw her more on buses that I did in life. For a small boy whose destiny was show business, I'm surprised I wasn't more excited, when I first encountered it. On one of our rare meetings my mother took me backstage of a show she was appearing in and introduced me to the cast. I remember a lot of very, very tall ladies and gentlemen, chattering a long way above my head. Someone famous called Lupino Lane gave me a mouth organ. Then the show started. I sat with my grandmother in the stalls. My mother didn't appear to have a lot to do. But I was quite concerned when she was captured by pirates. For my mother's part she took it quite calmly, frequently pointing me out to her captors. And I remember thinking: 'I bet she gets into trouble for that.'

The show ended with a lot of cannons banging and my mother winking at me as she paraded round at the end. And that was the nearest I got to show business for the next twenty years. That is with the exception of the Metropolitan Vicker's Works' pantomime at the Palace Theatre, Manchester. There was a pantomime horse with two men in it. Unknown to me it had been prearranged that the Dame in charge of the horse would ask if any little boy in the audience would like a ride. We all screamed, 'Yes! Yes! Me! Me!' The horse then walked down the aisle, led by the Dame, who asked the horse to choose a little boy to ride it. Needless to say, the horse lifted a leg and pointed to me. The Chief Engineer and Inventor obviously had a lot of pull. I was hoisted up on its back. Before the horse even made it to the stage, I was sick on its head. I distinctly remember somebody in the back half saying: 'Oh Calamity, its been sick.' I was ignominiously returned to my seat. Since then I've never been too keen on surprises.

When the long summer holidays arrived, I used to look forward to the Saturday morning visits to the cinema to follow *The Adventures of the Lone Ranger.* I used to gallop home, beating my backside with a rolled-up comic, saying, 'Come on Silver!' Another favourite was *The Adventures of Flash Gordon*, who travelled in futuristic vehicles. The idea of the future depicted by artists in those days made it seem quite an attractive time to look forward to. There was always a mad professor; a villain with a spiked helmet; a spacecraft looking rather like a submarine with a fire-work attached to it, heading for the outer planets or invading the Earth. Now I've arrived in the future, I find it rather disappointing.

Between the air raids, Toy Town, the Lone Ranger and Flash Gordon, the War seemed a perfectly normal world to grow up in. Night-time was particularly exciting because trucks would tow guns up and down the road in Didsbury, firing into the sky, while the searchlights poked white fingers into the sky looking for the enemy. I remember seeing the glow of Manchester's Ship Canal Docks going up in flames; the uneven drone of enemy planes and the scream of bombs coming down. It all seemed very exciting to a small boy. And I was always loathe to be dragged down to the shelter. One really never expected it to change.

By now, I was rather good at roller skating. A gang of us would meet and roller skate for miles. In those days the skates had metal wheels. And clickety-clacking over the pavements could send you numb to the knees quite quickly. We were also very keen on soap box racing – that is to say, we would find an old pram, remove the wheels and get the local greengrocer to give us a wooden packing case. We would make a wooden beam front axle, attach two pieces of rope, and steer ourselves at high speed down any convenient hill. There were some high sand banks along the River Mersey. Its black, silent waters covered with mountains of soapy bubbles, the smell is still unforgettable today. But to us it was exciting to take off at the top of these sand cliffs and hurtle down, fortunately, stopping short of the water in which none of us would have survived for more than thirty seconds. We got to know the River Mersey quite well. I'd walk for miles along the banks with my friends, throwing stones, and taking it in turns to push each other in our home-made death traps, always looking for a steep bit of bank to fly down.

On one of our riverside excursions, we found an enormous fair in progress – the sort of thing you only see now on old films – with boxing, a sleeping princess, and a bearded lady. Plus a two-headed man. I remember being suspicious about the two-headed man, because only one head ever spoke. But we were very gullible. We paid to go in and see him three times. The reason we did this is that the second time the other head spoke, but the one that had previously spoken remained silent. It was only on the third visit that we realized that the heads had been swapped round. We were so fascinated by this that we got masks and some stuffing and made extra heads for ourselves, which we pinned onto our shoulders. We went out cycling with them, hoping that people would be impressed. My grandmother said she thought it was disgusting and made me throw mine away.

During this time, we moved to quite a nice big house in the best end of Didsbury with an orchard and a summerhouse, which was ideal for playing toy soldiers in. We had a big front garden with a high hedge. I remember the local toy shop,

Inman's, selling high explosive toy bombs. These had special exploding caps in the nose. Hiding behind the hedge, I'd wait for a pedestrian to pass, throw it over the hedge and wait for the bang. This often resulted in a ring at the doorbell, but by then my grandmother was rather deaf, and before I undertook such an adventure, I was careful to disconnect her hearing aid.

I had become quite fascinated with the adventurous life I saw on films and often tried to emulate it. Usually with disastrous results. Encouraged by one epic, a perilous adventure where a group of climbers had a tough time on the north wall of the Eiger, I found a rope and fixing it to the pedestal of a wash basin, climbed out of the third floor window and proceeded to scale down the side of the house. I reached the drawing room, jut as my grandmother entered. She was very surprised to see me outside the window, particularly as I suddenly disappeared, due to the fact that the hand basin had become detached with the strain on it. Fortunately, I landed on a rhododendron bush.

My next visit was a film involving parachuting. I could hardly wait to get home and get my grandfather's golf umbrella and leap out of the first floor window. I had the good sense to try a sandbag on it first. The speed of its descent, and the collapse of the umbrella, convinced me it wasn't one of my best ideas. Nevertheless, I was still game enough to attempt the long flight of stairs from the top landing on a tea tray, with grandma's best cushions positioned against the wall at the bottom. It is amazing the exhilarating things you can do indoors on a rainy Tuesday.

In those far off days, I was often sick, and whenever I found myself home on a Sunday, Grandpa would take the family car, the faithful Rover Ten, out for a spin in the country, either to pick blackberries or to buy fresh eggs – or indeed any excuse to exercise his driving skills. We used to go to a farm where, in those days, they had wonderful old-fashioned threshing machinery, all horse-drawn. I have a vivid picture of a farmer banging away at rabbits as they ran out of the corner that was being threshed. We used to come home with home-made bread, milk and jams. I must say all the food used to taste a lot better then. If it was raining, we'd still go out and have a picnic in the car: a thermos of tea and some sandwiches. And we would just look at the countryside through the windows. On these journeys I was always put in the back seat, because I couldn't do more than twenty miles without being sick. My grandmother constantly had her head screwed round, looking at me, until she'd shout: 'Stop Sydney! He's gone green.' The car would screech to a halt; the door was opened and I would oblige them. It was a Sunday ritual. I remember a trip to Blackpool when I was sick four times going and five times coming back. It was only some years later, when I drove myself, that I realized that my grandfather belonged to the jerky school of driving. And in cars driven normally, I am perfectly all right.

Before I leave life in Didsbury, I must mention Great Aunt Louie, who bore an uncanny resemblance to that master of B movie horror films, Boris Karloff. Despite her forbidding appearance, she was probably the most kindest, and certainly the most generous person, I have ever met. Cursed by fate to be single, because of her slightly unprepossessing appearance, it was said she had been extremely popular with men when younger, mainly due to her remarkable generosity. This was only possible, because her father, Great Uncle James, had been bedridden on the top floor of their rather grand house and was unaware that his daughter was busy selling off the contents below, floor by floor. This was in order for Auntie to maintain an active social life. Apparently dear Auntie Louie was in a constant state of nerves, in case Great Uncle James ever recovered enough to stagger downstairs. Fortunately for her, he never did. When his coffin was carried out from his well-appointed bedroom, it descended down carpetless stairs, past empty rooms in which every scrap of carpet, ornament and curtain had been flogged off, through the front door and past the space where the umbrella stand used to be. By the time I met Auntie Louie, she was already on what they call 'hard times' and was a lady's companion. Bouts of dizziness caused her to disengage herself from this occupation from time to time to stay with relatives. It was always an exciting experience when Auntie Louie would arrive.

I can recall my first meeting with her. The doorbell rang and on the doorstep was a taxi driver wrestling with a giant ship's cabin trunk, and leaning on a malacca cane, was Auntie Louie, smelling strongly of mothballs, dressed in black-flowing clothes from head to foot, topped off with a large hat. She was a vast woman and had teeth the colour of rather faded piano keys. My grandmother welcomed her warmly and I was introduced. I also got my first glimpse of her financial acumen as she borrowed two pounds from my grandmother, gave the taxi driver five shillings, gave me half a crown and put the rest in her handbag. Apparently this was quite normal; my grandmother explained to me that, although she didn't actually have any money to spare, she was very fond of buying presents. Half a crown was a small fortune in those days. I loved Auntie Louie immediately. I still loved her six months later, as by now, she was tipping me handsomely for doing little errands, such as running to the shops to buy chocolates for her and flowers for my grandmother, and writing paper and stamps, so she could correspond with other relatives, requesting sanctuary and also answering advertisements for 'A Companion Wanted'.

She seemed to spend a lot of time in bed, but occasionally she came downstairs and had dinner with us. Auntie Louie's hearing aid was a much older model than Grandma's and was pinned just below her voluminous bosom, looking rather like a small radio set. A long wire dangled in a loop and was caught by a brooch on her shoulder, allowing the plug to be fixed firmly in her ear. My grandmother's was a slightly different arrangement. She used to wear her receiver inside her blouse; one was never quite sure where it was. The wire popped up from her collar and disappeared into her hair. It was quite interesting watching a conversation between the two of them: Auntie Louie would speak to different parts of my grandmother's body, hoping for good reception, and my grand-mother was constantly bent down, shouting at Auntie Louie's bosom. And then if they got too near together, they'd both get a bit of static and have to retreat.

On the occasions that Auntie Louie did attend dinners, I was always amazed at her prodigious appetite. She could demolish as many helpings that were going. And should there be a piece of bread left anywhere on the table, she'd take it and wipe her plate clean. Her conversations with my grandmother were wide-ranging, covering such topics as the bowel move-ments or lack of them in other relatives, to the tragedy of Scott's last expedition to the Antarctic. Bombing raids were still in progress, of course. Quite often, Auntie Louie would have to be helped down into the cellar. This was always an exciting experience, particularly after dinner. She had a remarkable capacity for passing wind whenever called upon to exert herself. This meant whenever she went upstairs or downstairs, or indeed, just got up from a chair. This sort of thing is very amusing for small boys and I remember being in a state of hysteria a lot of the time and being told off by my grandmother. 'She doen't know she's doing it,' she said. 'So you mustn't laugh.'

One night, after dinner, I unpinned the receiving end of Auntie Louie's hearing aid, and repinned it on her posterior before she went to bed. I then turned the volume up to full and waited. Actually I didn't mention this to my grandfather or my grandmother, but I remember the event clearly. As Auntie Louie got to about the third stair, there was a loud raspberry. Auntie paused thoughtfully, then leaning over the bannisters announced that she thought a storm was brewing. Oh happy days. I was very sorry when she left. She did, however, manage to borrow my entire weekly pocket money, just before her departure, in order, she said, to be able to send me a birthday present the following year. I couldn't complain. Thanks to her I had more toy soldiers, when she left, than when she arrived.

On the rare occasion, now, when I smell mothballs, I have

a vivid picture of those piano-key teeth, of her black bombazine clothing and the creak of her stick as she would ascend the stairs, farting her thanks for another splendid dinner. Needless to say, as she got larger and larger and less mobile, relatives started playing Russian Roulette with her, each hoping that they would not be the last one to be left with her when she was incapable of leaving the house. Apparently she got as far as Norwich before this happened, where she passed away, leaving a cabin trunk full of party dresses for a much slimmer figure, severe black companion's outfits, dressing gowns, bath towels, slippers, an enormous address book and a few hundred mothballs. Clearly, she was an invaluable relative to have had in the fabric of one's life, particularly for a writer who has to make up characters. Luckily, I have one or two to call upon that need no exaggeration.

I had an excellent opportunity to study characters in my school holidays as my grandmother positively enjoyed taking me to the shops. She seemed to know everybody and I suppose my subconscious must have soaked up a lot of the dialogue. I remember we would spend half an hour in the butcher's; and if I was lucky, he'd give me a couple of rib bones, which when cleaned up, and held between the first and third fingers of my right hand, could produce quite a good tune as I rattled them. I had been taught to do this by one of my grandmother's brothers – Uncle George, I think, who had been a member of a minstrel group. I don't think they exist today, but in those days they would put black boot polish on their faces and sing things like, 'dem bones is driving me crazy'. Apparently the sound of me practising on my bones didn't please my grandfather too much either and I was always made to do it in the garden.

We would then have a long stint in the greengrocer's; the chemist's, where if I was lucky I would be given a couple of pence to go to Inman's Toy Shop, while my grandmother did a bit of window-shopping. She was an expert window-shopper. I think this was because she only had a very small allowance and never liked to go in, unless she could actually afford to buy something. We used to peer into a lot of windows; it was probably quite unnerving for the assistants. She then spent at least ten minutes, deciding whether she could afford some fifteen denier stockings or not.

She was also very selective in the people she stopped to chat to in the street. To avoid people she didn't want to talk to, she would incline her head and keep on walking. When describing this action later, she would say, 'I moved to Mrs Sortel this morning, but we didn't speak.' Mrs Sortel, needless to say, 'moved towards my grandmother'. As my grandmother seemed to know almost everybody in Didsbury, a lot of 'moving' used to go on and a simple visit to the shops, only minutes away from the house, to buy some sprouts or false teeth adhesive, could take a whole morning. It might sound boring for a small boy to spend a lot of holidays like this, but I never found it so. My grandmother always seemed so proud to show me off to her friends.

'This is Eric,' she would say, 'I mean Harold, I mean Jeremy.' She always had trouble with my name. 'He's in private boarding school.' Then she would mouth, 'but he's a bit backward.'

Then they would go into code.

'Is his father still . . . ?'

'I'm afraid so . . . '

'Does his mother ever . . . ?'

'No I'm afraid not . . . Although she did briefly last year . . .'

'Does he still, you know, in the car . . . ?'

'Every journey, but I always know when it's about to happen and we always stop in time . . . '

'How long will he have to wear that . . . ?'

'Oh, until his other eye gets stronger . . . '

'He's very thin, isn't he . . . ?'

'Yes, we've got him on Virol to build him up. I don't know why he's so undeveloped. I blame it on the fact that his father only had one . . . Here's tuppence, go and look in the toy shop.'

I never found out what my father only had one of. Every

time the conversation came up, I was always able to buy a toy soldier or a bag of sweets. Then we would trot off home, both 'moving to people', two or three more chats, and if I was lucky she'd take the route that crossed the wooden bridge at Didsbury Station and let me wait for a steam train to pass underneath. There is nothing like the thrill of being completely shrouded in steam when you are small. It smells just like Swan Vesta matches. I still use them today to remind me of it. I don't want you to think that in these reminiscences I found life boring in the slightest. In those days we created our own excitement. Particularly when I constructed the world's largest catapult: double-strands of quarter-inch elastic afixed to the fork of a defunct apple tree; the actual sling being the inner sole of one of my grandfather's golf shoes. And I found some splendid ammunition in his tool box in the shape of quarter-inch ball bearings. As a test run I aimed at a crow, standing on the chimney pot of a house quite a few hundred yards away, I let fly. The crow remained unmoved; the complete top window of the house disappeared in slow motion with an audible crash. I hurriedly removed any evidence of this remarkable weapon, ran indoors, complaining of a headache, and went to bed for the afternoon, waiting for a visit from the police. It never came.

2

My grandfather died while I was still at school. I was informed that he was ill and, arriving home at the beginning of the holidays, I remember seeing a flower petal on the doorstep and I knew right away that he was dead. I can still see my grandmother standing in the bathroom, putting her lipstick on crookedly, while she cried. He was only about sixty, and she had loved him very much. I think she was quite glad she had me to look after.

The house was sold and my grandmother decided we should go to London to stay with a distant relative, near Wembley. Another school was found for me called Orley Farm, a rather posh establishment which was a sort of prep school for Harrow. In fact, it was just a bit further down the hill. Sadly though, I was unable to make the next quantum leap from the lack of education at the Doctor Thwackum Academy in Cheshire to the sophisticated curriculum of Orley Farm. So my father decided it was pointless spending money on any further education and retired me, roughly at the age of thirteen.

He did this long distance, as he was busy fighting Rommel in Africa. He was a young Captain in the REME, rising finally to the rank of Lieutenant Colonel. Unfortunately, we didn't get on too well. I was always rather frightened of him. He was brave, daring, handsome and intelligent. All the things I wanted to be. It was only later he became an alcoholic, bad-tempered and irascible, which were all things I didn't want to be. But life in wartime Wembley, in the upstairs apartment of the distant relative's house, was great fun. The bombing, the searchlights, the general excitement of war, finding schrapnel in the streets and the dense fogs, which we used to have in those days, provided a constant atmosphere of excitement. Made more exciting by the fact that I didn't have to go to school. I became very good at making models in plasticine and would construct twenty or thirty members of the German Army, scoop out the backs and fill them with tomato sauce. Placing them in a strategic position at the end of the garden, I would shoot them from long distance with a telescopic-sighted air-rifle. Very realistic, I must say.

The bombing in London seemed to be twice as severe as in Manchester. We had direct hits in one or two houses quite near by and could still hear the din of guns going off on their mobile carriers and the scream of bombs. It was quite hectic. Then there was the excitement of the doodle-bugs; I actually saw one of these as it flew overhead. When the engines stopped they used to nose dive to the ground. Often we would see vapour trails as the Spitfires and Hurricanes battled it out with the German bombers and their escorts. I was never aware of being afraid. Although I'm sure that was due to not understanding how serious it really was. I remember Grandma coming home one day from shopping with torn stockings, saying she had had to throw herself down in the street as a German pilot had tried to machine gun her. I'm sure he didn't actually have Grandma in mind. But there were one or two low level attacks where the streets of London did get sprayed with bullets.

On one of his brief visits home, my father decided that my puny frame would be improved by taking up a life on a farm. I was duly sent to a farm in Egham in Surrey, where I joined in the hay making, the milking, and became very friendly with the local rat-catcher, who said he would be happy to teach me the trade. I must say rat-catching can be fun. I know it doesn't sound like it: prowling about farmyards at night with a stick and a dog, with the thought that at any moment a large rat might land on your head from a hay rick. But it certainly kept the already highly trained adrenal glands going. There wasn't a lot of entertainment in the mid-nineteen forties, apart from the radio, a wind-up gramophone and of course, horses.

It was on that farm I first learnt to ride and to love horses. They kept quite a few. But amongst them was an old racehorse called Ostrich, a grey of about fifteen hands with quite a turn of speed left. I used to take Ostrich down to Runnymede where the Magna Carta was signed (this knowledge was the direct result of a Doctor Dunwell beating) by the banks of the Thames. Ostrich would gallop till we were both exhausted. We were great friends. I often discussed my life with Ostrich and Ostrich would go to sleep on my shoulder. I suppose my life was rather boring for an ex-racehorse.

The war ended and my father came home and bought a house in Stoke Poges. I was invited to reside there. By now he was married to the girl he had run off with: a perfectly nice lady called Nan. And nearby lived great friends of theirs called Mr and Mrs Mills, of the Mills Circus family. As a result of this, I attended the circus quite often and was privileged to meet the last London to Brighton coach driver, not unsurprisingly called 'Old Tom'. 'Old Tom' was in his late nineties, and helped look after some of the animals. He was a splendid old gentleman with a merry twinkle in his eye. Tiresomely enough, he couldn't remember a thing about driving the London to Brighton coach. A bit of a disappointment as far as history went.

I had passed no exams at all in my life to qualify me for any sort of work at all, and it was clear that living in my father's house was getting on his nerves. He got in the habit of introducing me to his friends as 'Dead Loss', son of Joe Loss, the famous dance band leader. All very amusing stuff, but not too good for the morale. Then Christopher Wren, the great architect, came to my rescue. He had built, amongst many other places, a wonderful house called Stoke Court, a vast edifice of thirty or forty rooms, with a cannon on either side of the front door, and a beautiful ballroom with french windows which led onto a terrace where the residents would take tea in the afternoon. From that terrace all one could see was a beautiful lake, surrounded by woods and an archway into the woods that led to a mile-long walk through the trees, known as Gray's Walk. You climbed a small incline and at the top of the walk was a maze, rather overgrown, but great fun to try and find your way round, and standing outside the maze you could look down on Stoke Poges Village. The walk was known as Gray's Walk, because Thomas Gray, the poet, had walked round it, then sat on a seat looking down at the village and had written one of his best poems from this very spot.

Stoke Court was furnished very much in the manner of a grand country house. In the winter there was always a big log fire burning in the hall with lots of comfortable chairs to sit in and of course, the inevitable radio. The cellars were full of croquet mallets, discarded golf clubs, flintlock pistols and cross-bows. In fact, a small boy's paradise.

As I was barely fifteen, this seemed a reasonable place to end my short life in and it was still only 1945. I remember my mother did pay me a visit there and took me up to London for the day. We went to Piccadilly and found an indoor amusement arcade; we were the only people there, apart from the attendants, and I was allowed to drive a Dodgem car round and round as she chatted to them. Then I was put on the train and sent back to Stoke Court. I think that it was probably the most I saw of my mother during the War. But I did enjoy Stoke Court enormously. There was a library where I voraciously devoured everything from Kafka to Mrs Beeton's early cookery books, one of which informed the reader that should the lady of the house pass an open fire and set her skirts aflame, she should pull the bell rope for the servants and roll on the floor in a table cloth until help arrived. There was even a clear instruction on how to remove a small stone or object that a child might have pushed up a nostril: get the child to inhale pepper up the other nostril and then pinch it shut. This guaranteed that the unwanted object would be exploded out. Fascinating stuff. These books, together with copies of *Punch* dating back to its first issue, kept me busy on rainy days; when it was fine I would fish the lakes or stalk squirrels with a crossbow. I never actually managed to hit one, but I left a lot of arrows sticking out of trees and it fulfilled the primitive urge to hunt that has all small boys in its grip.

In the evenings I sat around with the elderly residents, all of whom seemed to have led very interesting lives. I remember one heavily whiskered gentleman had been a submarine commander in the First World War. 'Whiskers' had been trapped at the bottom of the sea, when he had ploughed into an old wreck; only by firing a torpedo had he been able to blow himself free. I thought it was the most amazing story I had ever heard. I wondered why everyone else wasn't as entranced as I was. It was only when he told it every night, I felt it lost some of its integrity. Nevertheless, Stoke Court was a fascinating place to live. It had a wonderful old ballroom with a wind-up gramophone with a very strong spring. As I was one of the few people strong enough to wind the gramophone, I was very popular with the older ladies who took it in turns to teach me ballroom dancing. I remember dancing the Blue Tango with a very elegant lady in an empty ballroom lit by a chandelier with the endless darkness outside the tall windows. The sprung floor would creak as we whirled round and round and somehow at that moment I knew that, once again, she was young and beautiful and I danced whenever she wanted to.

Occasionally I would see my father – he only lived a few hundred yards away. Usually when he went to play squash on a court in the grounds. Then he would retire to the bar with his partner for a drink. He would ask me how I was. And I would say I was well. Then he would ask me if I had decided yet what I wanted to be or do. And I would confess that I still had no idea – although I was good at fishing, reading and dancing the tango.

On one of his visits he told me that he had bought an interest in a firm of home maintenance engineers and that I had at last got a job. I was to be a plumber's mate. I was to report to the plumbing firm the next morning where I would be given overalls and taught a trade. This news came as a cultural shock. For by now some eighteen months had passed, and I had adopted many of the mannerisms of the elderly people with whom I had been living. Often I affected a tottering walk and I was rather good at collapsing into chairs. As instructed the next morning, I climbed on my bicycle. Yes, I had a bicycle. Things weren't all that bad. And I pedalled off through the Christopher Wren gates and headed for Farnham Common. On the way I stopped to watch a film crew. They were making a film of one of the *Just William* books. I can't remember who was playing William, but I do remember being rather envious of the small boy who was playing the part. William had always been one of my favourite characters. I'm not sure how the real William turned out. But I don't suppose he became a plumber's mate. I did. And I can't recommend it.

The plumber, whose mate I became, was called Shrapnel Boisey Smith, a huge man, with a red face and tattooed arms. 'We'll soon toughen you up, son.' Shrapnel obviously had received instructions from my father. 'Grab them lead pipes, tank cutters, Stillsons, the tin of boss white and hemp and we'll be off in the van. We've got a job in Slough on the trading estate.'

The various items were pointed out to me and I carried them to the ramshackle van, which grandly proclaimed that not only were we plumbers, but also heating engineers. We arrived at the Radio Café in Slough. A sort of pit stop for truck drivers. We climbed to a small area full of pipes and a large metal tank somewhere under the roof.

'Now your first job, as a plumber's mate,' said Shrapnel, 'is to take this tin paint kettle, wash it with white spirit, and polish it with sand paper till it shines like bleedin' glass.'

'I say Shrapnel, old chap, why are we doing that?'

'So's we can have our bleedin' tea in it. That's a mate's first job, making the tea.'

While Shrapnel attacked the hot water system, I did my best to make the paint kettle shine like bleedin' glass. By lunchtime, I thought I had succeeded. Shrapnel reached in his tool bag and produced a box of sandwiches.

'Where's yours?' he said.

'I didn't know I had to have any.'

'Better get down to the caf' and get some and get the kettle filled up with tea. Bring it back up here.'

'Right ho, Shrapnel. I say, is this what's called starting at the bottom?'

'Definitely my son.'

I went down to the café, handed the paint kettle to the young man behind the counter and said, 'Hello, old chap, would you mind filling this up with tea.'

A deadly silence seemed to descend on the Radio Café. The bespectacled plumber's mate, in pristine overalls, seemed to be the centre of attention.

'He's a right comedian,' said a voice.

The surly looking young man behind the counter leant forward and confided that he didn't like the look of me. I replied that I didn't particularly like the look of him, but I did need a paint kettle full of tea. Before I had time to mention that I had a weak heart, he was across the counter, punching me in the face. I stepped back, got my leg tangled in a chair, and fell backwards across a table. By now a circle had formed to watch the entertainment. It wasn't the sort of friendly fight you have at school. The word *pax* seemed to have no meaning in the Radio Café.

'Shrapnel,' I shouted. 'Help!'

I remember seeing my aggressor's nose within inches of mine. Like a wild animal I snapped my teeth shut on it and hung on determinedly. His shrieks of anguish indicated I had made a deadly enemy for life. Shrapnel appeared and pulled him off. Shrapnel obviously realized he had made a bad career move sending me down to get the tea. After that incident, life with Home Maintenance was fairly quiet. I became quite an expert at climbing on roofs to replace tiles, sawing through pipes, replacing lavatories. Not to mention, a dab hand with the blowtorch. All of it was good experience for a future career as a writer. By now Shrapnel and I had become quite good friends, although I did nearly kill him. One day I was up on a roof, while far below Shrapnel was holding the ladder. I had half a pound of putty over from the job and casually threw it over my shoulder. I climbed down to find an unconscious Shrapnel spreadeagled on the lawn. After that my putty was rationed. One thing was certain plumbing was far more fun than school. Well certainly the ones I went to.

One of my jobs was in Eton High Street, digging up somebody's front garden to repair a drain. I was on my way to the local Chip Shop for lunch, when I passed one of the old Etonians, who stopped and gave me a second glance.

'Good heavens, Jeremy Lloyd, isn't it?'

'It is, indeed!'

'What are you doing in that outfit?'

'I'm a plumber's mate.'

'Good heavens, that sounds fun.'

'It is,' I said.

He seemed completely unshaken by my lowly occupation and I remembered meeting him at Stoke Court, when he had visited his grandparents a year or so before. We had had quite a long chat in the grounds where he had found me fishing. We shook hands, he touched his topper and sauntered off. I rather wish I had gone to that school. But then I would have missed a lot of experiences yet to come in the real world.

3

About this time my father and his second wife parted and he moved into a room in a pub called The Crown, near Burnham Beeches. No longer able, or willing, to sustain my small room at Stoke Court, my father suggested I should go back to live with my grandmother, who had taken rooms in Rickmansworth over a bank. They were very small and it always seemed to be damp and foggy in Rickmansworth. Thanks to my father's influence, I got a job in the Standard Range and Foundry in Watford as a metal sorter and counter hand. I paid seventeen shillings and sixpence for my first trilby, kissed my grandmother goodbye, presented my workman's season ticket at the station and started, once again, where I belonged – at the bottom.

Metal sorting does not require a lot of intelligence; it does, however, require a pair of industrial gloves. Unfortunately the early morning Rickmansworth fog, followed by metal sorting, did not agree with my health and I became quite unwell, and to my father's dismay had to take early retirement. By now a number of my grandmother's relatives, and friends, had decided it was time they died. And my main occupation seemed to be accompanying her to funerals. She always looked very smart in a veil, and seemed to consider these occasions a 'day out' as they say in the North. In between funerals, I managed to do some fishing in the local reservoir, and occasionally we would visit my father's brother, Harold, and his wife, Marjorie, who lived in Pinner. I still visit them today, and I am delighted that they are still hale and hearty, as they are my dearest friends and always give me a warm welcome.

Grandma then became quite ill and I became a male nurse for some two or three months, until we both decided we had had enough of Rickmansworth and Grandma spent the rest of her savings on a modest semidetached house in Northwood. Not the best end, but not the worst, and near a very big house where the diveway always contained a collection of old cars.

These belonged to Derek Wootton who had just come out of the Air Force. Wootton was an absolute nut about vintage cars, building specials up from bits and pieces, and racing about in the countryside in them. We became firm friends and are still so to this day. Petrol was rationed then, so he just used to make his own with methylated spirits and mothballs. It only needed a leaky exhaust pipe for us both to turn purple and pass out in some country lane. But this was my first taste of real adventure, racing about in cars and I loved it. And I couldn't wait to build my own, which with Wootton's help, I did. It was an Austin 7 which blew smoke rings past the starting handle, but it was mine and suddenly the road stretched ahead and I felt the first taste of real freedom before I fell unconscious from a leaky exhaust pipe.

Just at that point, the government ordered me to report for National Service. My father, naturally, was very excited. I was not personally overjoyed at the thought of going to Korea to confront the enemy, but in those days one did what was expected. And kissing grandma goodbye, I turned up at the recruiting office, ready to do my bit. By then I was six foot three and weighed nearly a hundred and twenty-two pounds. I was congratulated by the recruiting officer for turning up, given ten shillings to get a taxi home, as it was raining, and was pointed out to the other recruits as an example of what can happen to you if you don't take care of yourself. I arrived home, just as my father called on the telephone to find out what regiment I was in. I told him the bad news: that somehow the army was going to have to do without me. This would no doubt prolong the war, but could not be helped. He was not amused. Grandmother was very relieved. Now I could go and get a job and help pay the mortgage off, which was already being assisted by a gentleman brush salesman, who had taken up residence in the front room which had been turned into a bedsit. But what job could I take?

My father stepped out of his Wolsley motor car, wearing a large camel hair coat and a rakish hat, looking not unlike Rex Harrison. We had tea and discussed my future.

'Well Chum, have you decided what you would like to do?'

'Not yet, Daddy.'

After the retirement home, plumbing, metal sorting and a quick affair with the military I was as undecided as ever.

'In that case,' said my father, 'I shall decide for you. My best friend, Mr Butterworth, is the managing director of the Ediswan Electric Company. I'll see you get a job there. It's in Charing Cross Road, in London. Naturally you'll start at the bottom.'

'Naturally,' I said. It would clearly be a misuse of power for me to start anywhere else. I duly appeared at the Ediswan Electric Company and was consigned to the basement to be a lamp bulb inspector, and occasional counter hand. I was also part of the unloading crew. That meant I had to stand in a cellar while boxes of lamp bulbs were thrown through a trap door from a great height. It would be unfortunate to miss one. I missed two or three and was moved to the shipping department.

By the way I am not making this up. There is such a thing as a lamp bulb inspector: you look at them and you run your hands over them. And an expert like me can tell you roughly how long they have been used for and if somebody is pulling your leg trying to return one. It is a very useful trade to have.

I haven't actually used it lately, but it is always there up my sleeve in case I need it.

Anyway, back to the shipping department. I had a problem working out the mathematical complexities of shipping tons, weights and measures and for some reason I had to learn a bit of Spanish. Due to my lack of education, I could never get the cargo to fit into the ship. So I was consigned to be a ship's runner. I was given documents which I had to get to the shipping offices in the City of London *tout de suite* without a bus fare. This was probably the best exercise I had had since I was at school. I used to get down there with bills of lading in double-quick time and be able to relax and have a coffee and read the paper before I ran back again.

I suddenly found a successful career at the Ediswan Electric Company: I became captain of their table tennis team. That was one thing I was really good at. I was an elastic-limbed demon at the table! We used to travel with our bats in their cases and boxes of competition balls on the Underground. Complete with our score books and special shoes we would arrive at Wapping Gas Works, or Lily Whites, and take on their teams. It was great fun. I was master of the top spin and the chop. An attacking player could drive me yards away from my end and I would always chop it back. That was in practice. When it actually came to the match, I used to go to pieces. Yet take away the responsibility of winning, I could beat anybody. But isn't it amazing how one can lose one's eye for a ball? I was in a house recently where they had a table tennis table and a child of eight beat me hollow, whilst I floundered around looking for my chop and top spin that seemed to have been left behind in a black and white world, which didn't move into technicolour until I started my life in show business.

By now I was about twenty-one and still had no idea of what I wanted to do. But at least I wanted to do something that I had chosen myself, and not something that my father had chosen. So I applied for a job at Simpson's in Piccadilly as a suit salesman. 'You'll have to start at the bottom,' they said.

And I found myself at the factory in Stoke Newington, sweeping up and helping to load garments as they came from the workroom. I didn't learn much from this except it was unwise to enter a lift full of factory girls, unless you were wearing a strong belt and braces, and could prevent them pressing the stop button between floors. Three months of this daily excitement and I was in the Men's Department in the main shop in Piccadilly, learning all the expressions; the most memorable one being, 'I'm free'. This was to become an invaluable asset some twenty years later.

In those days there was a pecking order in the gentleman's ready-to-wear department that must be apparent to even the casual observer. A customer will appear at the top of stairs, the senior salesman glances in his direction and looks towards the floor walker for approval to walk forward to accost this potential customer. The floor walker will nod and the senior assistant will walk forward and say, 'Are you being served?' Another useful phrase. As he does this, the senior assistant will assess the customer's spending power, and if it doesn't look very good, he will pass him on with a nod to the second senior assistant, who may well pass him on to the third or the fourth. I was the junior. I would only get people who came with holes in their shoes. Quite often these people had pockets bulging with cash which used to annoy senior assistants considerably. I was a very good salesman. Frequently using the phrase 'Don't worry, the sleeves will ride up with wear to cover the fact that the jacket's too long'. Or indeed doing what they call 'kneeing it' – that is when a jacket is too tight. You would say, 'I'll just look for another one, sir.' Then you would take it out of sight, put your knee in the arm hole, break all the stitches, and bring it back, saying 'Is that more comfortable?'

'Yes, that's fine.'

'Good, it's the last one we've got.'

'I'll have it.'

Simpson's will deny this, of course. Nobody has ever kneed a jacket at Simpson's. Perish the thought. Getting into the spirit of things, I started to wear smart stiff collars and stiff cuffs: a dozen or so a week, revitalized by the steam laundry at Watford, and returned to the house by van. Travelling to work I wore a rather natty felt hat and even arrived one morning with a walking stick. This was considered to be extremely jumped up by the senior staff. Subconsciously I suppose I was emulating the elderly gentlemen at Stoke Court, where I had actually learnt to use a walking stick properly. It is an art, wielding a walking stick, there is a rhythm to it. I would wield my walking stick down Piccadilly to and from the Underground looking, I thought, very debonair. I probably looked a twit. My father came to see me; he bought a pair of trousers and informed me he hadn't told any of his friends I was working there, as he considered it not a proper job. It was a bit unfair and I had got him a discount on the trousers. He suggested I should take up night school and probably learn maths or something like that. Something useful. I said I would consider it.

I went to the Polytechnic and studied the courses and chose sculpture. Twice a week, I threw mud at a wire frame, trying to copy Michelangelo's David, a small replica of which was on a stand. I made something which I christened neolithic person and resigned in disgust. I was disappointed that a hidden talent had not been revealed to me. I was still optimistic about my hidden talents when I visited a great aunt who had a grand piano. I sat down and hit all the keys as hard as I could in the hope that a concerto might emerge. All that emerged was the great aunt who pulled me away and slammed the lid shut, informing me that I should never touch the piano again. But you never know unless you try.

My home life had become most enjoyable, because with my friend Derek Wootton I was enjoying rallying in cars – driving through the night, clutching a map and bouncing up and down, occasionally having to use a cycle pump to keep the pressure up in the petrol tank of an Austin 7, as we climbed a steep hill.

In those days I had never even heard of St Moritz or St Tropez, or ever thought of going to Los Angeles; never dreamt I would be sitting on a beach in Barbados or dancing under the stars in Mexico with Merle Oberon; or writing for Danny Kaye and acting with the Redgraves; or engaged to Charlotte Rampling and married to Joanna Lumley. All of which happened much later. I hadn't even started writing yet. And when I did, it came about in a rather strange way.

Since I had written three episodes of the Red Mask in about 1937–8, I had not had the urge to write anything except a thank you letter for a birthday present or the word 'Barouche' on the bonnet of my first Austin 7. But my next occupation changed all that. I found that there was nothing worse on a lovely summer's day than wearing a tight stiff collar and a hot suit, standing in a gentleman's ready-to-wear department, waiting for people in their summer clothes to come in to look for more summer clothes. So I found an occupation more suited to see some of those fine days before they passed forever. And I applied for a job as a paint salesman on the Ruislip Trading Estate.

I must mention that at about the same time I had joined the local tennis club in Northwood and met a very charming girl called Dawn, who was the daughter of the local curate. Having played with her regularly for two years, no pun intended, we became engaged, then married and moved into a small apartment in a suburb of Harrow. She worked at Liberty's as a model together with other regular house models. I would take various chums there to lunch and the models would parade past the tables. If they saw one they liked, my wife would effect an introduction. Two or three of them got married as a result. I even thought of starting a marriage bureau; I was always trying to think of something to do . . .

But back to the trading estate at Ruislip. What I was after, you see, was the salesman's car and the open road, and the opportunity to knock on people's doors and sell them paint. Not that I knew anything about paint. But paint couldn't be very different from suits. This paint was; it turned out to be commercial industrial paint to prevent rust and I was asked by the Chief Chemist what science degrees I had to enable me to understand the complexities of this product.

'None,' I said.

'Good day,' they said.

On my way out I took a product leaflet, walked into the factory next door and sold them fifty gallons of paint. I went back with the order and asked again if I could have the job. I think they were rather astonished, particularly as the paint I sold was very expensive. I was given six pounds a week, and a boarding house allowance for when I travelled out of London, which usually meant a trip to the Midlands to look at some factory where rust was rampant. I became an expert at selling rustproof paint. One of my best sales was to get the railings in Regent's Park painted grey. You probably remember them. It was around 1954. It didn't last long. They turned brown by 1956. When it rained, I would go to the cinema. I became very conversant with every film that was on. I would put in a report saying, 'Went to the Tate and Lyle factory today, had to wait three hours for an appointment.' Needless to say, if it had been raining I would have spent the three hours in the cinema.

But the most memorable thing about representing industrial paint is the smell at the factory; this is all pervasive and it needed a number of baths to get rid of the aroma of pungent hydrocarbons and chlorinated rubber. Grandma was very thrilled I had got such a good job and lent me three hundred and fifty pounds to buy a Ford Popular motor car, my Austin 7 being too unreliable. I immediately had ten thou' removed from the cylinder head, special valves and pistons put in, a straight through exhaust and the front suspension modified. This increased the performance from sixty-two miles an hour to nearly sixty-five. And it certainly made it more fun to drive.

I was given a pack of visiting cards, which announced that

Mr J. J. Lloyd was an official representative of the paint firm and was an expert in anti-corrosion products. I'm afraid the card wasn't very impressive as it was typewritten. I complained about this and was told if I wanted better cards I would have to pay for them myself. I did. I ordered fifty with raised lettering and generally improved the layout. I also bought an India rubber, as my meetings were mostly with factory foremen who would take my card and peer at it and then hand it back with a great big thumb print on it, which of course I rubbed out to extend the life of my cards. I was also handed a sales pack which consisted of a list of names and addresses of customers or would-be customers, a pile of sales brochures and an impressive card which was painted with an acid-proof coating: this was so I could demonstrate it's ability on the spot, should I find myself for instance in an electroplating works.

'Drop some of that acid on this card,' I would say. 'And you'll see how good our paint is.'

Six times out of ten the card would curl up and vanish altogether. And on the occasions when it resisted the attack of the chemical, I would do my best to sell gallons of the stuff – to paint all the machinery, the floors, the walls, the ceilings, and anything else that I thought could be done. Most electroplating shops have duck boards that you walk about on, but I visited one or two rather more primitive ones where I found after I had failed to sell any paint, the soles of my shoes had burnt off, while I was doing my pitch. I don't know what the aftereffects of inhaling all those fumes might be; I am still waiting to find out, as I spent a lot of time in fume-ridden factories with acid rain dripping from the roof. There is nothing more disheartening on a cold winter's day than standing at a factory gate using the gateman's phone and announcing that you have come to try to sell some paint.

'Could I please see the works foreman?'

'No, leave a card.'

When that happened, I would just leave one of the typewritten ones. I used to visit a lot of factories at Ponders End in

North London and was a frequent visitor to Barking Sewage Works, where the firm's paints were permanently being tested to see if they could protect metal work from the ravages of sewage. I remember having to park my car about half a mile from the Chief Sewage Engineer's office, and walking past endless sewage pits, before entering his hermetically sealed office where dozens of bottles of Airwick were strategically placed. It was always a fruitless mission. Whatever samples I had left, they would fail to withstand the ravenous hunger of South London sewage. I must say it was a bit of an eye-opener, going to sewage works. Once I found myself deep down in the bowels of London, gazing in horror at an iron-grating as it was raised up from one of the fast-flowing sewage rivers that run beneath London. Trapped in a grating was the body of a premature baby. I gathered it wasn't an entirely uncommon occurrence.

On another occasion I was sent down to Greenwich to investigate a buoy, which had been painted with anti-rust paint and situated at a place called Dead Man's Reach, an inhospitable no-man's-land part of the Thames. I was taken in a small motor boat to investigate this large rusty metal cylinder as it lay silently in the water. Before the boatman could stop me, I stepped out off the boat and stood on it. To my horror, it started to roll very slowly under my feet. And I started to walk to keep pace with it. The motor in the boat failed; the boatman tugged unsuccessfully at the starter rope a few times, until the river swept him away, out of sight round a bend. So I was alone, walking just above the water, smartly dressed in a bowler hat and a smart suit and, if I can recall correctly, I still had an umbrella hooked over my arm. I was a bit dapper in those days. A ship's hooter sounded, and around the corner came a German cargo vessel, with *Bremerhaven* written on the bow. The first sight of anything really English, which I'm sure they remember to this day, was a bowler-hatted gentleman walking on the water, waving at them and saying, 'I say, hello there.' One does have a sense of occasion for these sorts of things. The last thing they saw, of course, was a demented person bouncing up and down in the wash, crouched on all fours, grasping onto a chain. Quite a highlight in an otherwise boring day.

Due to my lowly position in the firm, I was also elected to be one of the van drivers. This meant having to take large drums of paint down to the docks in East London. It was a rotten van and was always breaking down. I can't say I enjoyed my visits to East London docks that much. I remember I narrowly escaped death when I approached a number of dockers, who were standing in a circle gazing upwards. I suppose I had assumed they were in some form of meditative trance. As I got to the middle of the circle, one docker threw himself at me; the force of his rush carried me to the outside of the group, just as the enormous boxed cargo landed in the middle from a great height, suspended from a crane.

I was also very nervous trying to find a café for lunch in areas like Cable Street, although I wore a van driver's dustcoat and cap. I always felt I looked a bit incongruous. Though sometimes it was quite good fun. I remember getting into a heated discussion with a group of dockers about the possibility of life on other planets. And I made a point of eating my peas off my knife, so as to be one of the 'in' crowd.

If I had been unfortunate enough to go to university, then decided to write, I would have been writing about these sort of people by guesswork. As it was, I had a lot of first hand experience. First hand, because I was indeed a worker. Although I clearly always had ideas above my station. I can recall being in a travelling salesman's guest house in the North. Sitting up in bed, in a tiny bedroom with a chamber pot in the cupboard, and carpets that didn't encourage you to walk on them in bare feet, smoking a woodbine and reading the social column in the *Daily Express*, I didn't know any of the people they were talking about, but it was nice to read about the goings on of the rich and famous, anything to escape the drudgery of peddling paint. I had no idea that I might well be appearing in the aforesaid column myself.

As a result of my life on the road and the increasing number of rainy afternoons in cinemas, I began to get the idea that I might write a film, since I seemed to have a pretty good idea of what was going to happen before it actually occurred. So one day I parked the car, and got out my salesman's notepad and started to write a film about the Loch Ness monster, which I called *What A Whopper.* I think it took me about two weeks: stopping the car and writing another bit of it, until finally I went to visit a factory, near Slough and found myself driving past Pinewood Film Studios. I drove up to the gate and asked to see whoever was head of the studio.

'Mr Earl St John,' said the gateman. 'And he does not see anybody without an appointment. Good day.'

I went to the nearest phone box, put the money in and asked for Mr Earl St John.

'Hello,' I said. 'I'm Jeremy Lloyd, I've written a film. They won't let me in to see you. It's infuriating, because it's brilliant, it's original and it's in my best writing!'

'Have you had tea?' said Mr St John calmly.

'No, I haven't,' I said.

'Are you a professional writer?'

'Not exactly. I'm a paint salesman.'

'I see. Would you like to come and have tea now?'

'Yes, I'd love to.'

'I'll phone the gate.'

An hour later, I was still sitting in his palatial office. I had read my story to him. I had also read it to somebody else that he had called into his office.

'We like it,' said Earl St John. 'We're going to buy it. Mind you, it's not very good, it'll need other writers.'

'I expect it will,' I said. 'It is my first attempt.'

But it was made and it starred Adam Faith. Whenever we meet, we both nod and smile. He knows it was my first attempt and I know it was his. Well, in the film world, anyway.

Encouraged by this success, I started writing to the BBC and everybody else I could think of, sending ideas in. Nobody ever replied. One day I went to dinner with some friends, where a very engaging man was playing the guitar and singing very amusing ditties. His name was Jon Pertwee. I could play about two tunes on the guitar, so I picked his up and played them and having established a rapport, told him that I was interested in writing.

'What have you written so far?' he asked. 'Because I'm looking for a new writer, mine's just left me.'

'Oh really,' I said. 'I've just written a major movie for Pinewood.' A slight overstatement, but at the time, it didn't seem to matter.

'I'm not sure I can afford you,' he said. 'I pay twelve pounds a week for rhymes and I'm due to do a piece on a television show called *Six Five Special* for a producer called Jack Good. It's hosted by Pete Murray. You've heard of him, of course.'

'Yes, of course, I have,' I said.

'Would you be free to write my material?'

'Oh yes I would, of course.'

'I live in Chelsea. Could you be there in the morning?'

'I could be there in the morning,' I said.

Next morning I drove my paint salesman's car to Chelsea, parked it outside his cottage, went in with a notepad and pencil and literally took down every suggestion he made. He would like to arrive on a chauffeur-driven tandem; he would like to do the following jokes; he would like to exit on the following line. I went home and bought a typewriter. I found I couldn't type, and persuaded a neighbour to type it for me. I returned with my version of what he had said.

'Come with me,' said Jon Pertwee, and took me to the BBC to meet Jack Good, the producer.

'This is my writer,' said Pertwee. 'He's just written a major film at Pinewood.'

'Ah,' said Jack Good, 'our writer has just left us. Could you take over the post?' He mentioned a figure that was ten times what I was getting a week as a paint salesman.

'That will be fine,' I said. It's amazing how calm I am in these circumstances. I think it's called temporary paralysis.

I handed in my keys to the paint firm. They regretted my leaving, and assured me that had I stayed on, by the time I was sixty I could be in a managerial position. I told them how much I had disliked the smell of their paint, and I was delighted to be leaving. I had entered the world of show business, never to return, or only in my worst nightmares, when I dream I am travelling about the countryside, selling paint. And I can't find my customer address cards.

4

Six Five Special ran for a couple of years, while I was writing it. Freddy Mills the boxer was one of the hosts. I got to know him quite well, and was very sad when I heard he had been found shot outside his club some years later. He was a gentle man.

Television was starting to take off, and at ITV they had a young up-and-coming producer called Brian Tessler. I heard that Brian Tessler was looking for new acts and new writers for a show to be called *New Look*. I was one of the many writers that sent ideas in; I still couldn't type, but I paid friends who could. I remember turning up at Brian's office in The Strand in my little Austin 7, wearing an ankle length raccoon coat and a deerstalker hat. I always tried to look funny in those days. Naturally I looked a twit. I thought if I looked funny, my work would sound funny. Jamming on the brakes as somebody crossed in front of me, I found I was unable to release them, and I was stuck in the middle of The Strand. Four policemen arrived, picked up the car and carried it to the curb. It was a good opening, I thought.

I sat in front of Brian and his pretty secretary and read all my jokes and funny sketches. He listened impassively. But, out of the corner of my eye, I could see her laughing. This is

44

going well I thought. Then a very jolly looking gentleman joined us, a stout fellow in every sense called Major Grafton, who was both agent and writer. And also the landlord of the Grafton Arms in Strutton Ground, Victoria Street – a pub made famous by Peter Sellers, Spike Milligan, Harry Secombe and Michael Bentine, and the others, who had evolved the famous Goon Show there, overseen by Major Grafton. It turned out that Major Grafton was going to take on any new writers that Brian found and they would be part of his stable.

This show was to have a number of new artists I had never heard of called Bruce Forsythe, Roy Castle, Baker and Douglas, and Lionel and Joyce Blair of whom I had heard, but then who hadn't, and Ronnie Stevens *et al.* At this time Jimmy Grafton was also writing a show called the *Billy Cotton Show,* which was to play a part in my life as well, although I didn't know it as I sat in the office, reading my funny sketches. Then it was over – with the usual 'We'll let you know . . . ' There is nothing worse than waiting for that telephone call, wondering if you have got the job. You pace about the house or flat or telephone box. It finally came. Major Grafton would like you to report to the pub at Strutton Ground. You are one of the writers on the new show, *New Look* to be made at the Wood Green Empire every Saturday night. Boy, I had arrived. I walked through the crowded bar of the Grafton Arms, up the smoky stairs, into the Major's office. Papers were everywhere. The Major was on the phone, making a frantic call. Was it to Harry Secombe, one of his clients? No, it was to the bookmakers. The Major was a keen backer of horses. 'Be with you in a moment Jeremy – just managed to get on the two-thirty with a Yankee double.' I was to find out that the Major spent more time placing bets than writing, and that doing the show in his presence was a laborious business, interrupted by the television set going on just as they were going up to the post, or the radio, or a call directly to the track. A lot of the writing was done in the attic. And it wasn't just *New Look*, it was any other show the Major was involved in. In those days we did lots of specials. Diana Dors appeared at the Wood Green Empire, with her husband Dickie Dawson. So we had to write a show around her. We did and found that in one of the sketches we were short of Tarzan. Would I like to play Tarzan said the Major. I said yes and he became my theatrical agent. In those days it was live television which is very exciting because you only got one chance to get it right.

I found myself in a loin cloth, swinging on a rope, shouting 'Hello, I'm Tarzan, but I've been ill.' Having got my cue wrong, I passed by Diana unnoticed. I swung back again, my nerves shattered, shouting, 'I've been ill, but I'm Tarzan.' I then let go of the rope and fell on her husband's foot. What he said to me later is unprintable.

I thought my show business career as an actor was certainly over. But this was not so. Although in retrospect, when I see myself on television in some old movie I sometimes wish it had been. But then I remember what fun they were and how lucky I was to have been invited into that club.

New Look was a great success and during its run the *Billy Cotton Show*, produced by Bill Cotton Jr, decided to look for an actor to provide some extra comedy. They were looking for a chinless idiot, a Hooray Henry type and as the gallant Major Grafton was busy writing the scripts, auditions were held in the Grafton Arms. I was brought down the ladder from the attic to act as a sort of role model, so the actors could get an idea of what sort of idiot they had to play. None of them quite came up to scratch and I got the part.

So for a couple of years I would appear on Saturday nights with a curly-brimmed bowler and an umbrella saying, 'I say Mr Cotton, I've got a splendid wheeze.'

'What's that?' Bill would say, gazing studiously at the rolling autocue, never taking his eyes off it, in fact. Something which I and other actors always found rather unnerving.

'I've got these two judo experts, sir. They actually look as though they're killing each other, but they don't hurt each other at all. It's an extraordinary skill. Could they put on an act here on your show?'

'Yer,' Bill would growl. 'Where are they then?'

And I would reply 'Oh dear, only one of them has arrived.'

'In that case,' growled Bill, 'as you know all about it, you'd better do the judo.'

And so I used to do strenuous judo and fencing acts and escapology, lead a rock group, or anything else that would seem slightly incongruous with my slim frame and personality. I knew I had arrived when taxi drivers would say, 'You're that twit on the *Billy Cotton Show*, aren't you?'

'Yes,' I would say proudly. 'I am indeed that twit.'

I used to meet other twits socially, who would say: 'I saw you on that show, gosh how d'you manage to be such an absolute twit?' I would reply in the same vein and they would laugh shrilly. 'Good heavens, that's frightfully good. How on earth do you do it?'

It was clear to me that being a twit and playing a twit is something the outside world found very hard to distinguish between. But emulating twits became quite a serious part of my life. As a result of my frequent appearances on the *Billy Cotton Show*, I was offered a part in a film called *School for Scoundrels* with Alastair Sim playing the headmaster of a school that taught unsuccessful men how to marry rich women or win at tennis. Or, indeed, anything to succeed. I had great fun working with Terry-Thomas, whom I got to know quite well; he was a most amusing and charming man. And is sadly missed.

During all this time, I had kept up my interest in cars. I think I must have had fifteen Austin 7s of various sorts and conditions and was still driving one in the days of the *Billy Cotton Show*. Although I had also acquired a Lotus 6, one of Mr Colin Chapman's first handbuilt racing cars, produced at his small factory in Hornsey. I became very friendly with Colin, who let me run in new cars, which I would drive through the night. By then I had a group of friends, who were all interested in cars.

None of us had any money really. And they would gather at the house I shared with my wife, Dawn, who would be in despair, when she arrived home from a modelling job to find the kitchen had been turned into a workshop and that there was an engine on the newspaper-covered kitchen table, as well as the floor, the hall-way, and most of the chairs. Motoring enthusiasts are not known for having particularly clean clothes or shoes. We lived in a world of oil and piston rings, punctuated by pints of best bitter, which is usually drunk through large hairy moustaches.

In those far off days the central point of motoring activity and beer drinking seemed to be the Denham Flying Club, where we would gather on a Thursday night to discuss our motor cars, play darts and listen to Whitington White and his sextet play 'How Could Red Riding Hood Have Been So Very Good And Still Kept The Wolf From The Door'. All innocent good fun. And if we were lucky, one of the members would offer to take us up in their planes.

I made friends with a chap who had a biplane called a Spartan *circa* 1920s. I remember sitting in the front cockpit while he flew from behind. We would take off, with bags of flour around my feet and fly very low over the Denham by-pass. Beneath us would be a friend driving a car flat out. In those days probably about seventy-five miles an hour. The object of the game was to hit the car with the flour bag. I had always been impressed by Errol Flynn in the film *Dawn Patrol* and this seemed like a re-run, with these death-defying antics which evolved into aerial dog-fights. We used to attach tubing to the top wings of the planes, then put rockets in them, and finally, with the adversary in view, light the fuses and watch the rockets whizz past. It was only when two planes actually collided that this splendid game was stopped. As I was in one of the ones that collided, I was quite relieved. We got locked together over Denham golf course and spun like a sycamore leaf as we came down (no parachutes of course), until the other plane, a Tiger Moth, broke away, losing part of its wing and landed safely, as we did. After that, such activities were prohibited. It was probably just as well.

In those far off days, one seemed to have a lot more fun than today. Mind you, in those days there were less people, which from the activities I have described is not surprising. My enthusiasm for engines and speed and the fact that I was working fairly regularly allowed me to purchase the Lotus 6 from Colin Chapman as I mentioned. It is worth about twenty times more today, if you can find one. In those days they had an 1172 Ford engine, with a special overhead valve arrangement. And I entered my first race at Goodwood with some confidence, having tried it out for about three months on the country lanes around Denham, racing against other friends with not unsimilar vehicles. In those days, there were no speed limits, in fact, police motor cyclists would often ride along side and say: 'Ello, Stirling. What can it do?' And you would tell them and they would laugh and say: 'Want to have a go?' And you would both have a go. I don't find the police so sporting today. They are usually more keen to show you their sophisticated radar equipment, which has just trapped you on the M3.

Anyway, as I say, I was very proud to have this Lotus 6 in polished aluminium, very fast and very light. It had the most exciting exhaust note, reminiscent of tearing calico. Goodwood was great fun in those days, and I remember arriving with Major Grafton, who had a country house nearby, together with a group of enthusiastic friends. The gallant Major had brought his cine camera with him and was going to film me as I negotiated the chicane, which in those days I seem to recall was the last tricky bit before you got to the straight past the stands. The opposition in those days would be MGAs, Austin Healeys, Morgans and that sort of thing.

As I sat on the grid, I heard the announcer say, 'On the second row, we have the twit from the *Billy Cotton Show.* It was clear nobody gave much for my chances.

I was confident, relaxed and I knew that I was good. I

hadn't taken into account that I was surrounded by demon enthusiasts, who had lightened and lowered their cars, polished their heads, tweaked their compressions, balanced their engines, made their own fuel and were determined to die or win on what was supposed to be a nice Saturday afternoon out. The only consolation was that the gallant Major Grafton had his camera relentlessly pointed at me, every time I screeched into the chicane and even when I came out backwards a couple of times. I wasn't quite last, although I should have been if a couple of cars hadn't actually blown up – that is to say their engines went bang and a lot of black smoke trailed out as they pulled off in front of me.

Nevertheless, it was a great experience. I couldn't wait to see it on film. I am still waiting. Unfortunately, the Major had recently photographed the eclipse of the sun and had put a dark filter in. All that could be seen was a dark shadow moving across the screen. I had risked my life for nothing. But the excitement of the day overcame all disappointment and this excitement remains even today, which must be at least a hundred and fifty cars later.

Life in the attic at the Grafton Arms in Strutton Ground went on endlessly into the night, day after day, with special material for Harry Secombe and Terry-Thomas, and then for the *Dickie Henderson Show*, to which I contributed: seventy or eighty shows, during which time I was allowed days off to act in the occasional film. Sometimes even longer. I found in show business one made lots of friends and it never seemed like work. In fact, I don't think I have ever worked in the true sense of the word, since I gave up selling paint. Writing and acting, and wrestling with ideas has always been fun.

I can remember, after doing shows, returning to London for a late night meal at Jack's Club in Orange Street, just off Leicester Square. Beneath this little club used to be a famous judo gym, run by the Robinson brothers, Joe and Doug. I got to know this place because during my time with the *Billy Cotton*

Show this is where I learned judo; in fact, I am still a black belt in origami! Anyway this little eating and drinking club was much frequented by the Crazy Gang. And so, on Saturday nights after shows at Wood Green, I would retire there with the gallant Major Grafton and one or two other writers for a steak and cabbage and hear endlessly funny stories from the wonderful members, who incidentally included people like Tommy Cooper. He was so hilariously funny that I had to eat before I spoke to him, otherwise I would get indigestion. It was there one evening I met the lovely Vivien Leigh, who was about to leave for Australia for her last and final appearance. I remember we spoke for about an hour and she was probably one of the most enchanting ladies I ever met. She had a magnetism, which unless you had been subjected to that sort of thing, would be hard to describe. I would certainly have followed her anywhere, had she asked me to. Fortunately, she didn't, as I was married at the time.

My late night forays, filming commitments and making the television shows kept me away from home a lot. And I couldn't say my marriage, certainly from my wife's point of view, was improved by my show business career. Then sadly her mother died, leaving a small amount of money, which we put down as a first payment on a rather large house near Stanmore. It was Victorian in origin with large rooms, which provided ideal entertaining space for the many friends I now had in my new career. Around that time, I had attended the Classic Car Show at Olympia, where a magnificent model slot car racing track had been erected and drivers, such as Stirling Moss and Graham Hill, and other great names of the day, were demonstrating their prowess on beautifully handcrafted model cars with electric motors. The track was about forty feet long and a replica of Brands Hatch. I and two hundred other car nuts gazed in awe, as the professionals put their cars through their paces. Everything from old racing Bentleys to Bugattis, to the latest Lotus. I *had* to have that track.

I went home, got a pickaxe and, despite my wife's protests,

demolished the intervening walls that separated one side of the top floor of the house from the other. The firm that had supplied the track to the racing car show arrived and erected the track. I also acquired the cars. Funnily enough, I was recently thumbing through a motor magazine and I saw my track described. The writer fondly remembering how realistic it was. The track became a social event: Roger Moore, who lived nearby, Michael Caine, Terry Stamp, and others, all came and played racing cars at the weekend. The house always seemed to be crowded and full of fun – a remarkably different life to the one that I had known before, and I seemed to have boundless enthusiasm and energy in those days. By then I had acquired a Lotus Elite, a rather sleek lavender job with red upholstery. My wife had a Triumph Herald and we also had a Mini. I still had an Austin 7 and the Lotus 6 tucked away in a friend's garage. I was living out my wildest fantasies and I was still in my twenties – and as I recall there still wasn't an official speed limit. Oh happy days!

My father had married yet again, not unsurprisingly to Mrs Mills, whom I'd met in the far off days of my youth, who even before she was Mrs Mills, was famous as Josie Leonard, partner of the World Ballroom dancing champion, Santos Cassani. I still see her occasionally today, dancing energetically on the top of an open bus with her partner on old newsreels of the twenties. I always remember her as a rather stern looking woman, who to her credit, did have to cope with my father's obsessive drinking habits and did so very well.

During all this time, I had seen very little of my mother, except for the occasional visit she made to London; about two or three in a period of ten years. My grandmother was living in a flat not very far away and I used to visit her every week. By now she was in her eighties and not in the best of health, but still charming and loving. My father had moved to a village in Buckinghamshire to become the manager of an engineering company that specialized in hotting up motor cars. So we were at least able to discuss the merits of various engines and the performance of cars, but I never got any closer than that to him. He still regarded my career as a transient phenomenon, particularly when he heard that I had been acting. He advised me against this, and pointed out that Laurence Olivier had recently had a very large tax bill which he seemed unable to pay. I am afraid I couldn't take his warning too seriously.

As far as my writing career was concerned, he did admit to seeing some of the shows I had written. The nearest he came to a compliment was to say: 'I didn't think the last one was as good as the previous one.' Unfortunately, he had never mentioned that the previous one was good. I seemed to be constantly on, as they say, a losing wicket. I think the fact was that he had had such a good time in the war when he was young, so that after the war his life seemed an anti-climax; and this, combined with the fact that I seemed to be enjoying myself with so little talent, clearly irked him. This may not be a fair comment, but I am sad to say I never seemed able to become his friend. As time progressed, his constant intake of the demon drink resulted in a number of visits to hospital to be dried out. I remember visiting him in one. Financially times were not good for him. And he asked if I could leave some money for him to buy the papers to read, in case I was mentioned in one of them. It was a sad moment, as I knew the only reason he wanted money was to buy a bottle. He wasn't that hard up. It was just an excuse. And to be nice to me for that reason made it an even sadder visit.

My grandmother had also become very frail and I was worried about her being alone in her flat, so I moved her into the Victorian edifice, into a comfortable bedroom, so that we could look after her. She had a wonderful memory. And although many of the stories were the same, I would sit in the garden on a summer's day and listen to her accounts of how in the 1870s, as a young girl she was run over by a horse-drawn tram and nearly had her left arm severed. This left it immobilized in a half-bent position, apparently the ideal angle

Listen very carefully . . .

for a golf swing. Though she had never taken the game up seriously.

She could also recall her mother's accounts of the troops returning from the Crimea. The residents of Ilford burnt barrels of tar to welcome them home. I am not sure why they burnt barrels of tar, but I had to take her mother's word for it. My grandmother could also recall clearly the first Zeppelin airship being shot down. Apparently my father was a young boy at the time, and with other young boys crowded round the wreckage. He returned home with a match box, in which he claimed was the little finger of one of the crew. He opened it in front of my grandmother and my grandfather to reveal, indeed, a finger. The fact that it was his finger stuck in the other end and painted with iodine and a bit of red ink did not allow him to escape from a severe thrashing for causing such a shock. He had a strange sense of humour, now I come to think of it.

I used to try to get my grandmother to remember any family history. But she was very vague, particularly where my mother was concerned. It seems my mother had quite a number of brothers, though I never met them. Nor did I meet her mother or her father, which was rather strange. By now my mother had also married again and had two daughters, who seemed unaware that I was related to them. When I did visit her at home, she asked that I should call her Margaret and say I was a friend of the family. I think she was embarrassed to have a son of my age when she had daughters who were considerably younger. I am not even sure they are aware of their relationship to me today. I last saw them at my mother's funeral some time ago.

Conversations with my dear old grandmother were sadly interrupted when I took her breakfast up one morning and she spoke a language I had never heard before, indicating that she had had a stroke. I pretended not to notice and spoke to her as though I understood perfectly what she was saying. The doctor confirmed that it was a stroke. And I cried a lot. I was really very fond of her. And although she remained bedridden, she did manage to recover some of her speech, but she became rather eccentric to say the least. She would hide her favourite bacon under the mattress, thinking somebody might steal it from the fridge. I once found her fighting the cat for it.

After one of my father's drying out periods, I also invited him to stay as well. He lasted about a week. Nothing we did seemed to cheer him up, although he did used to have long conversations with my grandmother, which usually ended in an argument when she berated him for his drinking habits. Then he returned home to catch up on them and was in a worse mood than when he had arrived.

It was at this time that I went for an audition for a new show to be made by American producers in England, starring Eve Arden, a Hollywood legend. I always remember seeing her in a movie where she sat on a piano and remarked: 'Oh, two octaves, I've got to lose weight.' She was a wonderful comedienne and had come over to make a series in England where she took over a Travel Agency and inherited the owner's twitish nephew, to be played by me. I was given the script which I learnt, turned up and did a screen test and was chosen for the lead. I signed a five-year contract with Screen Gems and went to Elstree Studios every day for about two weeks, to make a TV pilot called *Take Him, He's Yours*. The tape of this show is on my memorabilia shelf as I write. It is in black and white and I look about twelve, and I was actually about twenty-eight when I made it.

With my future assured, I took off for a holiday in the South of France in my lavender Lotus Elite with the red upholstery, followed by my wife in her Triumph Herald, which contained the luggage. We went with two other friends, who possessed one of the early E-Type Jaguars. I used to race with them for a hundred miles or more and then wait for my wife in the Triumph Herald to catch up. Pretty rotten of me, I suppose. But we did have a lot of luggage. We decided to spend the night in Monte Carlo. It was my first visit, and finding a small hotel, we decamped, and at my suggestion, headed for the casino. I had never been in a casino before. The one in Monte Carlo was quite breathtaking, in fact I think it was about my first trip out of England. And France has always held a fascination ever since.

At the casino I proceeded to play roulette. The game does not require a lot of intelligence. But certainly quite a lot of stamina. My stamina lasted until I had lost my share of the holiday that we had booked for a month with our friends. Our friends and my wife were appalled. Even with only a few chips left, I could not be persuaded to stop. I was still convinced I could break the bank. The holiday was in jeopardy and my friends refused to lend me any money to recoup. I suggested selling the Triumph Herald, but my wife refused even to consider the idea. And between hysterics informed me that her mother had been right, she should never have married me in the first place. I had been of the same opinion for some two or three years, but had not liked to mention it. In those days one didn't get divorced, one sat it out, until familiarity overcame individualism. Fortunately, fate has always played a great part in my life. I did meet a man I knew, who was prepared to cash a cheque for me. I went to the cashier, bought more chips and returned to the table. By now my wife was under sedation with alcohol; my friends had returned to the small hotel to continue the holiday on their own in the morning, and I sat grimly until the casino closed. I just about won back what I had lost. It was an emotional experience. After that, the holiday at the Villa Pelican, near St Tropez, was quite a success. I even learnt to water ski. And found some wonderful roads to drive my Lotus flat out.

One night we took a trip to Cannes, taking the Lotus and the Jaguar, we raced all the way there. My friends had purchased their Jaguar from a dealer in London. What they didn't know was that it still had fingerprint powder on it, as the police suspected it had belonged to one of the gang involved in the Great Train Robbery. Since its purchase the number had not been changed and Interpol had not been advised that the car had been cleared of suspicion. As we sat on the beach, outside the Carlton Hotel in Cannes, plain bathing-costumed police-men appeared from nowhere, arrested my friend and his wife and drove them back to the Villa for questioning. I followed in my Lotus Elite with my wife, who was once again in hysterics. We were both relieved to find that my companions had been cleared. But it is moments like this that really make holidays go with a swing.

I returned from France to find that the TV show with Eve Arden was not good enough to become a television series. I was very disappointed. I thought my chance to go to America had gone forever. But then I didn't know what was going to happen in my life. I thought I had reached the pinnacle of my career already, but it was not to be so. I was unprepared for the embarrassing 'down' moments just round the corner.

Back in England I continued writing the endless succession of *Dickie Henderson Shows*. Dickie was a wonderfully calm comedian, perhaps the most unruffled person I have ever met. The only time he ever showed any great surprise was when I announced to him that I was going off to Spain to do a night-club act.

'You on stage? Alone?'

'Well, not alone,' I said. 'I've got a friend called Rex Berry who wants to do it. He's very tall and very keen.'

'Has he ever been on stage before?'

'No.'

'Have you?'

'Well, apart from the *Billy Cotton Show*, no.'

'You mean a live audience in Spain?'

'Yes, we're entertaining at a hotel in a town called Estartit on the Costa Brava.'

'I'm very glad,' said Dickie, 'that I haven't your nerve in my tooth.'

I didn't realize quite what he meant at the time. I had

been talked into this venture by Rex who was bursting with confidence; in fact, he was bursting with everything. He was at least sixteen stone, wore enormous horn-rimmed glasses and was always sweating profusely. He was in the advertising business. In fact, there was hardly anybody one could ever bump into in those days who hadn't heard of Rex Berry. I am sure he was very good at advertising, because he absolutely oozed enthusiasm for everything he did. I met him the other day after a gap of nearly thirty years and the first thing he said to me, after he had clapped me on the back was, 'Do you remember when we went to Estartit? Wasn't that amazing?' He was still oozing enthusiasm, although his hair had gone white in the meantime.

But I'll never forget Estartit; it was one of those decisions one takes out of pure ignorance. I had a phone call: 'I say, Jeremy, I've got a terrific idea, I think we should go to Spain and do a nightclub act. This holiday firm will give us a free room in a good hotel. It's on the beach, do say yes, it'll be great fun.'

'Hang on Rex, what sort of act do you think we should do?'

'They're grateful for anything out there, old boy. They're English holiday-makers starved of entertainment. You're a big hit in the *Billy Cotton Show*, there's bound to be loads of people there who'll recognize you.'

'Rex, I only do a three-minute spot on that show – a nightclub act could be a bit longer!'

'Don't worry about that, we'll think of some act. I've been on stage before.'

'I didn't know that. Where?'

'I did a play once in India, an amateur production in Bombay. Can't remember the title but I was very good.'

'You never told me this.'

'I've done so many things, I sometimes forget. Anyway, let's meet and discuss.'

We duly met for dinner. Rex showed me the brochures of the hotel; they looked very nice. There was a small stage in the gardens, where we would be performing. The only thing missing was an act.

'Let's put our heads together,' said Rex.

We did. We came up with what can only be described in retrospect as badly judged material. It was to be two chaps in bowler hats and umbrellas singing thirties-style numbers, rather like an act called the Western Brothers. A bit posh, interspersed with my playing the guitar and singing the two or three songs that I knew, plus an impersonation I did for friends, of a mad rock and roll singer. Then Rex would recite 'The Green Eye of the Little Yellow God', while I hid behind him, putting my arms through his, and re-enacting the words as he spoke the deathless prose, such as 'He returned before the dawn, with his shirt and tunic torn . . . ' My hands would then tear wildly at his shirt. Rex would then announce there was 'Blood upon his brow . . . ', at which moment my hand would appear with a tomato and hit him on the forehead with it. Sounds hilarious, doesn't it? We saw somebody do it once and thought it would be a very good idea. We intended to end with 'Rule Britannia', but actually never got that far. We left on a tour bus and joined a package tour aeroplane. I had my guitar firmly in my hand throughout the whole journey. The plane was of course full of English tourists, heading for various parts of Spain. I always remember with a shudder a small boy peering over the seat in front of me and saying: 'Can you play that thing?'

'Of course he can,' said Rex. 'He's probably the most brilliant guitarist in England.'

'Stop bothering the man,' said his mother.

'I bet he can't play it,' said the child.

'Go on, play him something,' said Rex. 'Keep him quiet.'

'I don't intend to start playing for children on a package tour aeroplane,' I said crossly.

'This is your audience,' said Rex. 'You'd better get used to it.'

'Nonsense! We're a nightclub act! Children of this size will be in bed by then.'

'They could let him stay up late. Go on, play him something.'

'Oh, very well.'

I took the guitar in my left hand and started to strum with my right. Just then the plane hit an air pocket and we had a very bumpy five minutes in which I managed to miss the strings quite a lot. I sang a very disjointed version of 'Sweet Georgia Brown'.

'Can't play,' said the child.

I had no idea a live audience could be quite so unnerving. And although there was an audience at the *Billy Cotton Show*, my material was fairly cast iron. Here I was improvizing and failing miserably. Rex seemed quite unperturbed by this incident. He started to recite 'The Green Eye of the Little Yellow God' – the story of mad Carew for which Rex was perfect casting.

We arrived on a hot Spanish night, disembarked and got on a tour bus, where to my relief the small child and its mother got off long before our stop. In fact, we were the only two people left by the time it arrived at our hotel. The manager was very pleased to see us. He spoke to us in halting English, with a German accent.

'Come into ze office. Ve must discuss ze act.' He sat behind his desk. 'Now boys, vot languages are you doing your performing in?'

'English,' said Rex, 'we do it in English.'

The manager drummed his fingers on the desk. 'Ve are ninety per cent German, five per cent Spanish, little French, and ve haff only von English family – ze Boddingtons.'

Rex frowned: 'I see, well look, don't worry old chap, lots of the Germans have probably been prisoners of war, they're bound to have picked up a bit of the lingo.'

The manager was not amused. 'I am a German.'

Rex nodded, 'You haven't had any problems so far, have you?'

'Vot about ze French? You must do something in ze French,

and something in German, also in Spanish, of course you can do something in English for ze Boddingtons.'

'We're doing it all in English,' said Rex. 'Although I don't mind putting in the odd "Guten Tag".'

'Zat means Good Morning,' said the manager. 'Ze show is at night!'

'Well if we're going well,' said Rex, 'it could go on well past midnight, in which case it would be morning.' Rex always had an answer for everything. I was already feeling depressed and remembered Dickie Henderson's words.

The manager looked at my guitar. 'Ah.' He seemed slightly relieved. 'Ah so ze act is music. This is good.'

'Well, partly musical.' I said. 'I play the guitar and do a bit of rock and roll. And a bit of cod-Spanish wailing.'

'And I stamp my feet,' said Rex.

'Music is good,' said the manager. 'Music is universal. All peoples understand music.' He smiled at me hopefully. 'How many languages do you sing your songs in?'

'English,' said Rex. 'He only sings in English. And we end with "Rule Britannia". Do you have a pianist or anything like that by any chance?'

'Pianist!' said the manager. 'Ve have a whole orchestra. The act before you features one of the finest guitarists in Spain, Juan Garcia.'

'Perhaps we should go on first,' I suggested.

'Juan plays for three hours,' said the manager. 'You go on last.'

'Can we go to our rooms,' said Rex. 'Jeremy looks exhausted.'

'Ve have no rooms in ze hotel; you vill be sleeping in ze annexe.'

Rex brought out the brochure. 'I was told we would have these two single rooms overlooking the sea.'

'You vill be in ze annexe,' said the manager and rang the bell. A man came along. Rex handed him his suitcase, the man ignored it, and beckoned us to follow him.

We followed him for about half a mile, until we came to a small building, climbed a flight of steps and opened the door to a room which had no windows, just ventilation slits in the wall and two single beds.

'Good heavens,' Rex said, 'we're not sleeping in the same room.'

'*Sí,*' our guide said, nodding and smiling. He showed us how the light switch worked and pointed to a cupboard in which there was just a basin and a large cubicle with a primitive lavatory.

'This is a bit thick,' said Rex. The man smiled and held out his hand.

'Piss off,' said Rex.

'When you organized this trip,' I said, 'I agreed to come along because we were going to have two rooms overlooking the beach. Can't see a thing from this room. And there's rather a strange smell from the street.'

'Open drain,' said Rex. 'I noticed it when we were walking along. I meant to mention it to you, but you'd walked in it by then.' Rex placed his enormous bulk on the bed which creaked ominously.

'I rather wish I hadn't come,' he said and suddenly burst into tears. I was surprised, because he had always seemed such a resilient person up till now. He opened his suitcase and brought out a bottle of scotch. Pouring some out in a cup, he offered me a drink – we both had two or three. It seemed to make him feel better. I was beginning to feel distinctly nervous.

'I'm going to sleep in my clothes,' said Rex.

'So am I,' I said.

It was not the sort of room you would normally bother to get into pyjamas for anyway. It was more reminiscent of a foreign legionnaire detention centre. We woke up both stiff with cramp. Rex went to the cupboard for a shave, and I went out and bought some tomatoes for 'The Green Eye of the Little Yellow God' act. I picked some nice squishy ones. When I got back, Rex was stripped to the waist, still wearing his large spectacles, busy shaving in the mirror.

'I've got the tomatoes,' I said.

'Good show,' said Rex. 'We might as well rehearse. Stand behind me while I'm shaving. And I'll do the dialogue and you do the actions.' Rex started to recite 'The Green Eyed Yellow Idol to the North of Katmandu ... ' During this, we heard footsteps on the stairs, but didn't pause. The door opened and the manager of the hotel appeared: 'Good morning boys. Did you sleep good?'

'Shush,' I said. 'We're in the middle of rehearsals.'

He stood back and looked at us strangely: hardly surprising as Rex was stripped to the waist, with me standing close behind him. The bag of tomatoes was on the basin.

'Mad Carew had blood upon his brow,' said Rex. I picked up a tomato from the bag and hit him between the eyes with it. It stuck to his spectacles and remained there.

'Is this ze comedy?' enquired the manager.

'Yes,' I said. 'This is probably one of the best bits.'

'Vell, I just came to tell you, Boys, you have to pay for your meals.'

'I'm going to phone Horizon Tours the moment we get home,' said Rex, removing the tomato and washing his spectacles under the tap. 'I'm going to complain. They said it was all in.'

We had a light lunch that day, then sat in our room, rehearsing our lines. As evening approached we brushed our bowler hats rather thoughtfully before we put them on. There was no chance of our changing in the hotel, so we were going fully dressed in bowlers with our umbrellas and my guitar, plus Rex's castanets, a bag of tomatoes and some sheet music, which we were going to hand to the orchestra when we got there.

'We should have rehearsed all this with the orchestra first,' said Rex.

I agreed. 'We don't even know if they will play for us.'

'Well, they better had,' said Rex. 'Otherwise they won't have an act.'

We arrived at the reception desk of the hotel. 'There's a note for you,' said the receptionist. She handed the note over. Rex read it.

'Good Lord, it's from the Boddingtons. Apparently they've had some terrible tummy problem, but they're determined to come and see us and they're getting out of bed to give us a cheer.'

'That's very encouraging,' I said. 'I wonder how many Boddingtons there are?'

'There must be at least two, to be plural,' said Rex.

I must explain at this point that the hotel was situated on a cliff with a long path cut in the rocks which went down to where the entertainment was taking place. We could already hear Juan Garcia warbling wildly away in the distance to the accompaniment of stamping feet and strumming guitars. The song ended and we heard a lot of applause.

'Sounds like a good house,' said Rex.

It was only then that I noticed he was slurring his words slightly and sweating profusely.

'You haven't been drinking that whisky, have you?'

'Finished off the bottle, when you were in the loo, it's hardly affected me at all. Just given me a little confidence.'

'You're pissed out of your head,' I said.

'I am perfectly capable,' said Rex, 'of entertaining a bunch of foreigners.'

I wished at that moment I had never left England, or heard of Horizon Tours, or even show business. We went and stood at the top of a stone staircase. It was a beautiful night, the moon was out. Juan Garcia was wailing away again, feet were stamping, guitars were strumming, and they were coming to the end of yet another number. On one side of the staircase there were multi-coloured tropical bushes, and alongside the staircase was the electrical power cable for the lights on the terrace. There was an archway at the top, which Rex was leaning against.

'I must admit,' he said, 'that quite suddenly I'm not feeling on top form. I think we'll get through this as soon as possible. I've probably got a tummy bug.'

Juan Garcia wailed to a close, and a rather reedy voice with a Spanish accent announced that 'Tom and Jerry', the great English comedy duo would appear any moment. Right on cue, the wooden archway collapsed and with a wild cry Rex disappeared down the stairs. On the way he clutched at the cable which was in the undergrowth. The lights on stage went out, leaving only candles burning on the tables. With flailing arms and legs, Rex arrived on the stage, rolling over a couple of times and then sat up, with his bowler hat squashed down firmly over his ears. For some reason this got tremendous applause. It went on for so long, that a member of the orchestra was able to scramble up the steps and reconnect the electricity supply. Rex climbed unsteadily to his feet, as I watched with horror from halfway down the steps.

'Thank you,' said Rex. 'Merci, Dankey Shern.' And then, as an afterthought, 'Grazias. And now I'd like to introduce my partner Jeremy Lloyd.' He held out his hand, and gazed towards the stairs with a sickly smile. I wanted to run and pretend it was a solo act. Then somebody called out: 'There he is, it's the chap from the *Billy Cotton Show,* I told you so.' A handclap started. I walked down the stairs as calmly as I could.

A very tall Boddington was standing up, with a very tall Mrs Boddington and two small Boddingtons. The Boddingtons clapped even more furiously. 'We're with you, chaps,' said Mr Boddington.

'We need all the help we can get,' said Rex. And for some reason he started singing 'Underneath the Arches'; he clearly hadn't had time to give the musicians any music. And as we had never rehearsed 'Underneath the Arches', I had to join in, putting a hand on his shoulder and doing a short walk up and down the stage. Fortunately, I did know the words.

'That's Flanagan and Allen,' said a Boddington voice knowingly.

'Why are we singing this?' I whispered, and then resumed singing.

'It's all I could think of,' said Rex.

' "On cobblestones we lay. Underneath the arches, we dreamed our dreams away ... " '

I sang 'For Me and My Girl'.

'Jolly good,' said Boddington Senior and applauded.

'Thank you,' said Rex, 'and now as I'm not feeling too good Jeremy will play his guitar.' To my horror Rex marched unsteadily off the stage and joined the Boddingtons at their table. I sang 'Blue Suede Shoes'; 'Georgia on My Mind'; and 'You ain't nothing but a Hound Dog'.

'Damn good!' shouted Rex who had recovered enough to help himself to the Boddington's wine bottle. 'Keep going.'

I kept going for about ten minutes before Rex hauled himself out of his chair and joined me. 'And now,' said Rex, 'let's all sing "Rule Britannia".'

The Boddingtons stood and joined in. It was a remarkable experience for the other guests. I still have the brochure somewhere; it says amongst the acts appearing were 'Tom and Jerry' – the famous English comedians. Now hopefully forgotten by all concerned, except me and my partner, Mr Berry.

5

I returned to the South of France again, almost before I knew
it, to star in a film called *We Joined The Navy*, directed by
Wendy Toye. When I say star, I use the term loosely. I played
Lieutenant Dewberry, one of three naval cadets in the care of
Kenneth More. Some of the filming was done at Dartmouth
Naval College. I remember leaving the hotel in Torquay in
which we actors were staying and arriving at a river where we
joined other trainee naval chaps who were being taken across
to the College. I was in my cadet's outfit and there was a tough
old naval officer in charge of the boat, who told me to throw
my cigarette away, and straighten myself up. I leaned back
languidly and took a puff, knowing I was safe, obviously he
hadn't recognized I was an actor.

'What's your number, boy?'

I replied, 'Kensington Two-six-nine-seven. Don't call me
early as I'm a late riser.' This was a big mistake. He turned out
to be the physical training instructor and I and the other cadets
had to learn marching and it had to look real. He gave me hell,
particularly when I asked for a duster to put under my shirt as
my rifle was cutting into me. He then harassed me mercilessly
on the assault course. I was quite glad when the unit took off
for the South of France. It was a wonderful location in Ville

Franche, a charming village port between Nice and Monte Carlo. The other two cadets were Dinsdale Landen and Derek Fowlds, with whom I became very friendly, especially Derek who stars in *Yes Minister.*

Filming in the South of France sounds glamorous and I can tell you it is. As I said, the film is loosely based round Kenneth More training three cadets on an American air craft carrier and to make it exciting there was to be a revolution on an island and we were going to be sent in to quell it. The cadets were to become heroes, which of course is very easy in a film. In one scene we had to leap out of the sea as frogmen firing our pistols. Unfortunately, my air canisters were so heavy that I couldn't get out of the sea in them, and had to crawl ignominiously up the beach!

The filming seemed to go on forever in wonderful weather; the result might not have been a memorable classic, but it was certainly the best holiday I ever had. Kenneth More used to give great lunches; he was just like the character he played in *Genevieve,* always great fun and very kind to lesser actors. He certainly made the most of life.

One of the glamorous girls in the film fell desperately in love with Derek Fowlds. Dinsdale and I could never understand it, for Derek was always rather shy, and we were extremely out-going to say the least. There was a memorable moment when Derek was walking along the hotel corridor with us some distance behind him. Suddenly a door opened, a hand came out and Derek was yanked inside and the door slammed and we heard the lock turn. By morning he was engaged. Dinsdale and I offered to be best man over breakfast, but by lunch the girl had changed her mind and fallen for Terry O'Neil who was working as the Stills Photographer. This we could understand, because Terry has always been very attractive to girls. Unfortunately, all the girls started falling for Terry and he was shipped off back to England, so we could get on with the film. I'm sure he won't mind me mentioning this, as he was very young at the time and unaware of his full potential as a lady-killer.

I was also very fortunate that on a trip down the coast to Cannes, I had bumped into a friend from England, whose father was the executor to the estate of the owner of a beautiful yacht. The yacht had a full crew, a chef, a drinks cabinet, and everything else you imagined a beautiful yacht could have and was to remain anchored in Cannes until the estate was sorted out.

'Would you like to live aboard it while you're filming, and take advantage of its facilities?'

'Thank you fate, I would.'

I threw some great parties, and needless to say with such facilities, I was very popular. During filming I met David Warner, later to become famous as a Shakespearian actor. Then he was playing a very small part. Even smaller than mine. The Americans had smart boats to collect officers from the air craft carrier and used what they called bum boats for the lower ranks. As David Warner was playing a lower rank, he only ever left on a bum boat. I was playing a lieutenant, and though clearly not such a good actor, always left in great style, usually on the Admiral's barge. This used to annoy David Warner considerably. I can't say he was over-popular with the other actors. We were always making apple-pie beds for him and generally pulling his leg. Age has calmed him down quite a lot. I met him not too long ago and he seemed quite a nice person, if slightly tense. Although I didn't have a particular girlfriend at the time, I did become quite friendly with the Admiral's daughter, who had persuaded her father to let her accompany him on his trip, together with her pink Ford Thunderbird. We used to nip down to St Tropez in it on my days off. They obviously had a much better time in the American Navy than in the British one. Though I don't think it is quite as efficient. They did have one special day where the Admiral of the Fleet made a visit and the battle equipment was being demonstrated. As one of the guns tilted up, a shell fell out of the breach, rolled across the deck and nearly hit the Admiral. The actors who were all watching gave a loud cheer, saying, 'Hooray for the red, white and blue!'

Heady days, indeed. And once again, I found myself at the casino in Monte Carlo. This time it was to push our producer Danny Angel round the tables in his invalid chair. Despite being infirm he was a very jolly person, always smoking a cigar and never short of a quip. As I did so, dressed smartly in my best dinner jacket and bow tie, a note to Mr Angel indicated that I had attracted the attention of a certain Mr Joseph Losey, the well-known American film producer. The note requested that I join him at his table, and indicated that I appeared to be ideal casting for a part in his next film. Danny Angel waved me away, cigar in hand: 'Talk to him,' he said. 'It may be a good part.'

I joined a rather morose looking Mr Losey, who introduced himself and bought me a drink. He told me I looked 'interesting'. I immediately gave him my best and most interesting look. I would, he informed me, be ideal for a part in his forthcoming production. Had I ever played a homosexual? He leant forward and gazed at me intensely.

No, I said, I normally played upper-class twits, which I was busy playing at the moment.

'You'd be good,' he told me.

I lowered my voice slightly and thanked him for the offer and explained that I normally played rather manly twits, and was at present playing a manly naval officer. In fact I didn't think it sounded my sort of part at all. He offered me a screen test. I declined. I really was a twit. The film was called *The Servant*, and James Fox got the part. Who knows I could have become a serious actor?

Joseph Losey is well remembered also for *Accident* and *The Go-between*. But then, had I done *The Servant*, I might not have written *'Allo 'Allo*. Or gone to Hollywood to do *Laugh In*. Or burnt so many midnight candles with my best joined up handwriting.

By now it was the early 1960s. I returned to England to find that my marriage had deteriorated to the point where we parted by mutual agreement. I gave Dawn the house, which was only fair as her mother's money had been the down payment. To my relief, Dawn had formed a strong friendship with a close friend of mine called Peter Lee, whose family owned the Bon Marché on the Harrow Road and had a boat. Both Dawn and Peter were very keen on sailing and even our dog used to appear in photographs wearing a life jacket. He was a Yorkshire terrier called Winkle; I was never very fond of Winkle. The only remarkable fact about Winkle was that he lived to the equivalent age of 134. He always reminded me of a sort of mobile brush and appeared to live on a diet of my best shoes. This does not mean I am not fond of dogs, I am. Just like people, they are individuals. Winkle was extremely bad-tempered, and had what can only be described as remarkable breath. Winkle went with the house.

I headed for sanctuary at the Grafton Arms, past the barrow boys outside, shouting the price of their fruit and veg, through the smoky snug and up the lino-covered stairs into the paper-strewn office. Jimmy Grafton welcomed me with open arms and a bottle of champagne and said he was delighted to have me permanently on the premises. This meant that he could indulge in a lot of betting in the day, and have me available to work at night. I spent a lot of time being permanently exhausted. We were still writing the *Dickie Henderson Shows* and making specials at Wood Green. I can remember, even in those days, worrying that inspiration was about to run out. Morecambe and Wise were rehearsing one of my sketches. I heard them complaining that it didn't have a very funny pay-off. Where was the writer? shouted Morecambe; Get me the writer! shouted Wise. I went and hid in the lavatory and they came up with a very funny line, without my help.

I was still keen on cars, which as luck would have it, was the reason why I appeared in the film called *A Very Important Person*, written by Jack Davis, a very well-known writer of comedies.

My Lotus broke down in Bryanston Square. Taking the

bonnet off, I made a mechanical adjustment, and revved the car up noisily. A rather portly gentleman opened the door of number five to complain. Smartly dressed in a blue blazer with a RAF badge and tie, he had what can only be described as an extremely mobile face and literally spluttered with aggravation as he complained about the noise I was making. I apologized profusely and as I did so, he recognized me as an actor. Although years later, he confided he thought I was another, better, actor. He asked me in for a drink after I'd apologized and we got chatting. It turned out he had written all the Norman Wisdom films amongst lots of other screenplays and he had a great sense of humour. He recommended me for a part in his latest movie called *A Very Important Person*. I was to play a shot-down British air man in a prisoner of war camp with Leslie Phillips and James Robertson Justice.

Leslie and I remained friends for years after that movie and James Robertson Justice was a remarkable character – just as large in life as he was on the screen. Apparently he didn't start out as an actor. He was a falconer in Scotland, who was asked down to advise on falconry in a film. When he arrived in his 300 SL Mercedes with a falcon perched on his shoulder, he was offered a film part and never looked back.

Jack and his beautiful wife, Dorothy, are still today two of my best friends. They live in Palm Springs. And Jack is still busy writing. That's the great thing about being a writer, you never stop, unless the brain packs up. Everything else can go wrong, and often does. But as long as you can get to the desk, get the pen out, or get a finger on the typewriter, something usually appears. Anyway, my friendship with Jack also resulted in me appearing in another very popular film which he wrote called *Those Magnificent Men In Their Flying Machines*, which starred Terry-Thomas, and amongst others, James Fox. In fact, I was recommended for the lead and did a screen test. I failed to get the lead, but became very friendly with James Fox and told him how narrowly he had missed starring in *The Servant* and recounted the tale of my meeting with Joseph Losey. He was very relieved, he said, that I had turned it down. He had a great sense of humour.

I hadn't a lot to do in *Flying Machines*, but the location was great fun. The flying scenes were done at an old aerodrome at Bracknell where they built a replica of Brooklands Racetrack – about half a mile of it. There were lots of vintage racing cars to be used in the scenes, and because I was very friendly with Jack and the director, Ken Anakin, I was allowed to drive some of them down the airstrip, and then take off onto the banking. It was great fun. The aeroplanes were all made at a university. One of them was so light, it could only be flown by a small female. And early one morning, standing on the Cliffs of Dover, I watched them fly overhead, on their way to France in the Great Air Race. It was a sight I shall always remember. Little buzzing engines, tiny planes, *circa* 1910. And with my imagination it *was* 1910 and I was there in my blazer and straw hat. What a lucky chap!

I played a naval pilot, who flew a rather strange plane that could only stop when I threw an anchor out. However, the only flying I did was hanging in the studio on wires. But on the ground, the plane actually went. It had quite a powerful engine. Special effects had arranged a wire attached to the under carriage, and with the film crew in a truck driving alongside, I roared down the runway, having supposedly just landed and on cue threw out my anchor. I had with me Ken Anakin's dog, which also wore goggles. Unfortunately, the special effect went wrong and the plane nose dived into the ground, breaking off the propeller. I disappeared beneath the control panel as it collapsed, with the dog clutched in my arms. An ambulance roared into view, with a panicking Anakin on board.

'Is my dog all right?' he shouted.

I climbed out of the wreckage, holding him up. 'It's fine,' I said. You realize how big your part is, by how worried the director appears at your possible demise. But filming in those days was great fun. Big tents, full of food at lunch time: hot sausage and bacon sandwiches at seven in the morning and lots of laughs. I remember one morning sitting next to Robert Morley in the make-up room.

'I believe you have a line with me today, Lloyd?'

'I say: Look there, sir. It's the Japanese fellow.'

'Ah yes,' said Mr Morley, gazing at the ceiling with a faraway look. 'But of course you're not going to say it like that, are you?'

I do find that laughter is the panacea for most ills. And even when things have seemed a bit bleak, or indeed, down right rotten, I have always been able to laugh. Thank goodness. Although, as I write this, it doesn't seem to have been a bad life: so far, I was divorced, my ex-wife was happy sailing and I was working at the Grafton Arms, with time off to make films. What could be better?

It was then that Wendy Toye reappeared in my life. Would I like to audition for a stage musical called *Robert and Elizabeth*, starring Keith Michell and John Clements? This was the musical version of the love story of Robert Browning and Elizabeth Barrett. I had never been on the stage before, that is apart from my staggering success in Spain. So I was rather nervous about the idea, but flattered that I should be asked. As it was a musical, I knew I would be asked to sing. I got my tape recorder and my guitar and, after a few attempts, did a rather good recording of 'Sweet Georgia Brown'. I arrived at the Lyric Theatre with thirty-two feet of flex, an electric plug and an adapter. The stage manager held my arm as I waited in the wings for somebody who sounded rather good to finish their audition.

'Next,' said a voice.

'You're on,' said the stage manager.

I walked on and held up my tape recorder.

'This is Jeremy Lloyd,' said Wendy.

I shaded my eyes against the footlights and peered into the gloom and saw a small group of people, huddled a few rows back.

'What's your range?' said a deep voice, which I presumed to be that of John Clements.

'About row K,' I said.

'This is a serious audition,' said Wendy Toye.

'I'm sorry. Do you have a socket that I could plug this recorder into. I've recorded a song I thought you might like to hear.'

'We'd like you to actually sing it,' said Wendy, 'we don't accept tape recordings.'

'That's a pity,' I said. 'I was hoping to come and listen to it with you.' I must say they laughed. I had a discussion with the pianist. The only thing we seemed to have in common was 'Goodnight Vienna', which was the only song he could play that I knew the words to. I sang then, occasionally I even hit the note. It was perhaps the worst audition that Wendy Toye had ever seen, but nevertheless I got the part of Captain Cook, the young twitish cavalry officer, who is in love with Elizabeth Barrett's sister, Henrietta, to be played by Angela Richards.

We rehearsed singing and dancing for what seemed an interminable period. The show opened at the Palace Theatre in Manchester. It was a great success. Although I used to feel sick every night before I went on; apparently this was quite normal. Unfortunately, I also laughed very easily. And on the first matinée, I made the mistake of asking the conductor to point at me with his baton when it was my turn to sing, as I had great difficulty in counting notes. He agreed to give me a direct wave with his baton, when it was time to start. Much relieved, I went on stage. It was a hot afternoon and I was in the middle of some dialogue with Angela Richards, when a fly buzzed round the conductor's head. He waved it away with his baton; I saw it out of the corner of my eye. My God, I thought, I've forgotten my cue. I burst into song immediately, much to the surprise of the orchestra, who were busy having a snooze. It also came as quite a shock to Angela Richards, as it was a duet. I don't think the audience understood a word of it. But it got lots of applause. Matinée audiences are very polite in Manchester.

The opening night in London was a great success. In fact, we seemed to have quite a number of opening nights. And suddenly I found myself in a dressing room full of telegrams and flowers, and for a moment I was a proper acting person. I even joined an acting club, where actors went to drink in Shaftesbury Avenue. The only thing I can really remember was that mine host was Gerry Campion, who played Billy Bunter in a television series. I was amazed at how like Bunter he still looked.

On one occasion Marlene Dietrich came to see the show, and popped round backstage to congratulate the actors, and, in due course, arrived at my dressing room and congratulated me. I told her how much I had enjoyed *The Blue Angel* and found myself taking her out to dinner at the Pickwick Club. She was very charming and kept signing lots of autographs. I don't think she had a great sense of humour, but I was delighted to be seen with her and waved to people I knew, in case they hadn't noticed. I was rather disappointed that Lionel Blair wasn't there. He is very good with famous people. I remember I took Marlene home in a taxi, got out, gave my best Erich von Stroheim bow, and kissed her hand. I suspected I hadn't been as dashing in real life as I had been on stage. It was only when I got home that I realized I had forgotten to ask for her autograph. But she was the first screen goddess that I actually met and I was very impressed.

During the run of this musical, I was invited to a party, given by Andy Bronsburg, a film producer. It was quite a regular occurrence really, but this turned out to be rather special. There was a great group playing in the garden called the Kinks, who were very popular at the time. And I met a young girl with waist-length light brown hair and remarkable cat-like eyes, who was looking for her coat at about the same time I was looking for mine. I distinctly remember something like an electric shock as our eyes met. I suggested a dance; she suggested a coffee.

We went to the kitchen and started chatting. I must say if there is such a thing as falling in love instantly, I had. I offered her a lift home and we talked in my car till dawn. The windows were quite steamy by the time she got out. Shortly after that I moved out of the Grafton Arms and into her flat in Smith Street. Her name was Charlotte Rampling, one of the funniest, loveliest girls in the world. A great friend, a marvellous dancer, with a great sense of humour. In fact we seemed to go dancing every night. If a restaurant was opening, we were there; if there was a show opening we went to it. I was invited to the opening of the Pair of Shoes gambling club in Hertford Street in Mayfair. I took Charlotte along, and for some reason we got photographed sitting on a roulette table and appeared on the front cover of *McCall's* magazine with a caption: 'Decadent London'. We weren't decadent; we were just enjoying life. We also became engaged.

Charlotte got her first big break in the film *Georgie Girl*. I remember I spent my last hundred quid buying her a pony-skin coat for Christmas; she wore it in the film. Funnily enough, I saw the film on television the other day and wondered what happened to that old pony-skin coat: was it stored in a cupboard with mothballs, or worn in Eastern Europe as part of a relief consignment of old clothes? I was still appearing nightly in *Robert and Elizabeth* and it was then that I met Harold Robbins.

Charlotte had come to pick me up from the show and Harold Robbins had been in the audience. He came round to con-gratulate everybody and seemed to know that I was a writer. He was a small balding man with very intense eyes and exuded confidence. He was very charming. I think he also thought Charlotte was the cat's whiskers. Anyway he took us out to dinner and I discussed writing and various ideas with him.

A few weeks later I received a book with a letter from him, asking me if I would read it, and outline any ideas I might have for a film treatment. The book was a true story of American life called *The Day They Shook The Plum Tree*, which took place at approximately the turn of the century and was about an old lady who was a millionaire recluse and so mean that she wouldn't pay to have her son's leg looked at when he became ill, and he then had to have it amputated. Anxious to impress his mother, he built a railroad through Texas and found a cure for boll weevils which used to attack cotton. Needless to say this was not a subject I was particularly conversant with. However, I did my best, having read it, to provide what Harold wanted. A humorous treatment, which occupied ten or twelve pages. I sent it back to him. A week later, I got a phone call. He was very pleased with my suggestions, could I possibly come to New York to discuss it further. He wanted me to meet some people with whom he was forming a production company.

How could I? I was in a musical. I only had Sundays off. I mentioned my problem to Wendy Toye, who very sweetly allowed me to miss a Saturday performance; an anxious understudy sprayed his throat and took over and I took off for New York. I promised to be back on Monday in time for the show.

Still some hours out of New York, the captain announced that due to fog, they would be diverting the plane to Montreal in Canada. I found myself at the Hilton Hotel with a lot of fellow travellers who were signing in at the expense of the airline. I was paged to come to the phone. I picked it up. It was Harold, still keen that I should arrive. Unfortunately, there wasn't another plane until Sunday, and I had to return to London. I called Wendy Toye at her home.

'How's New York?' she said.

I explained I was in Canada.

'This could only happen to you,' said Wendy. 'You'd better go on to New York, dear, and try to get back on Tuesday.'

I must say there aren't many directors who would have said that.

I arrived on Sunday in New York to be met by Harold Robbins, who had me whisked through immigration in a second. We talked late into the night at the Plaza Hotel about the proposed film. The next day he took me to lunch at the Four Seasons; I had never been to New York before. It seemed to be full of steaming manholes, high kerbs, a lot of traffic, and neck-stretching skyscrapers. In the middle of the Four Seasons restaurant there was a sort of small swimming pool with fountains. Harold and I had a table nearby. He wanted to phone the coast – shorthand for Hollywood. He demanded a phone and told the maître d' to turn the fountains off, so that he could hear the coast distinctly. Harold was a very big noise in those days. The fountains were duly turned off. He spoke to the coast; I spoke to the coast. I am not sure what I said to the coast, but the coast seemed keen that I should work on this project. Harold assured them that as soon as I was out of the goddamned musical I would be down there.

After lunch we went to Bloomingdales.

'If there's anything you want,' Harold said, 'I'll buy it for you.' His royalties had provided him with an enormous amount of cash. And I was very impressed. I suggested, as it was rather cold, a pair of gloves, hoping my modesty would impress him. On the contrary: 'When I say anything, I mean anything,' he snapped. 'You've got to learn to be able to spend!'

'I promise to do better.'

He took me to his publishers and asked which of his books I hadn't read. I pointed to one and got an autographed copy of *A Stone For Danny Fisher*, making a mental note that I must start reading his works as soon as possible, in case I had to take an exam on them.

I promised as soon as I got out of 'that goddamned musical' I would fly back. However, there was no chance at all of being out of 'that goddamned musical'; it was a great success and was just entering its second year. But once again fate played the Joker.

In the mid-sixties I was asked to do a day's filming by Bryan Forbes. The film was called *The Wrong Box*, in which seven or eight lesser-known actors are killed so that one or two famous actors can solve the crime. Famous actors included Dudley Moore and Peter Cook. Not being a very famous actor, I only had a small part as a victim; I had to be killed in one of the opening scenes by cannon fire from my own side. I gave orders to fire, whilst still standing in front of it. A typically twitish thing for an officer at the Battle of Balaclava to do. I was ideal for the part. The cannon was duly rolled into view, accompanied by a special effects man, whose appearance, I must admit, did worry me slightly. He looked as though he had had some plastic surgery. What I didn't know then was that, it was rumoured, he had sunk a ship, lent to a film company by the Greek Navy, and blown up an aeroplane in Africa. But I did suspect he had had an interesting history.

Bryan asked for the cannon to be demonstrated; the special effects man lit the fuse. There was a loud bang. Part of Crimea, which was built at the other end of the studio, disappeared. Leaving quite a hole in it.

The special effects man apologized and said, 'There must have been something up the spout.' We agreed with him.

He was ordered to remove the gun and come back after lunch with a bigger one, as Bryan was not satisfied with the size and wanted a bigger bang.

We had an rather enjoyable lunch. I regaled the table with various stories of failure and returned to the set. Now there was a very large gun, probably one of the largest guns I had ever seen. The special effects man assured Bryan that it was all in working order; I squinted down the spout to make sure there wasn't a cannon ball in it. The special effects man said he was ready and winked at me encouragingly, with one of his better eyes.

'Right,' said Bryan. 'Stand in front of the gun. Everybody ready? Action!'

I stood resplendent in my officer's uniform, raised my sword and shouted: 'Fire the gun!' A soldier obeyed by lighting the fuse. The man behind the camera reminded me in mime to throw the sword away when falling. I held my sword up with a fixed grin for what seemed an eternity. There was a loud explosion, which propelled me upwards, engulfed in flame from my waist to my fur hat. At the same time sixty-two pieces of shrapnel entered the back of my head and the left side of my lower jaw. It was quite an exciting journey, and seemed to happen in slow motion. I have a vivid recollection of the first aid man, rising from his seat and striding purposefully in my direction. He fainted as I hit the floor. A nubile, dark-haired actress called Nicole Shelby, who was to be killed in a later scene, knelt beside me, cradling my smoking remains and screamed, 'For God's sake darling, say something!' She called me darling, because we knew each other quite well, or had done before I met Charlotte.

'Get the stills man to photograph my face,' I said. 'This insurance claim could clear my overdraft at the bank!'

After that, I remembered nothing else, until I woke up in Stoke Mandeville Hospital, where various bits of metal were being removed, without anaesthetic, by a very tall man, wearing big spectacles. He waved his tweezers under my nose and assured me he was a well-known plastic surgeon.

'We've got to get as many of these bits of rust out as we can,' he said. 'But don't worry, quite a lot of it is just gun powder burns.'

I was very relieved to hear that.

Heavily bandaged, I returned to the apartment I shared with Charlotte. I ordered her not to open the door, until I had explained what had happened. She was laughing so much, by the time she opened the door she forgot to faint, but she was very sympathetic. Naturally my stage career in *Robert and Elizabeth* was over. I phoned Harold Robbins.

'Hello Harold, I've got good news. I'm out of the play – I got blown up on a movie.'

Harold got down to business right away. 'Is the brain still working?' I assured him it was. 'Then get over here as soon as you can. I'll send a ticket.'

I couldn't go right away as I had to see the film insurance doctor, and also wait for an operation, but I promised to leave as soon as I was well enough.

The insurance doctor was very old and gave a weary smile. He had been through this routine many times before.

'Hello, how nice to meet you. Come in, sit down. My word, let's have a look. Good heavens, where is it?'

'It's here,' I said, angling my head, lifting my chin, and pointing to the back of my left ear, jaw, and general area. The doctor took out a large magnifying glass with a shaky hand.

'Let's have a good look, yes, I can see some slight marks there, all down the side of your chin. Makes you look a bit rugged. Pity it didn't get you on the other side as well. To have matched it up. You'd look better a bit more rugged.'

'I never wanted to be rugged,' I said.

'Has the accident affected your hearing?'

'I beg your pardon?'

He raised his voice slightly, 'I said has it affected your hearing?'

I nodded.

'Are you sleeping? Has it affected that at all?'

'Constantly affected; nightmares every night.'

'Really? What do you dream about?'

'Being blown up and never being able to work again.'

'I don't think it's quite that serious,' said the doctor. 'Have you been able to do any work since it happened?'

'Of course not,' I said, indignantly. 'Who wants an actor with a half-rugged face?'

'I see you're also a writer.'

'Yes, but I'm not suing about my writing career, I'm suing about my acting career.'

'Ah, so you can still write?'

I said I thought the motor region of my brain controlling my handwriting was entirely different to the brain area that was terrified by the thought of going on a film set again. I then noticed he had the pictures on his desk taken at the time of the accident. I picked them up and waved them under his nose.

'See how badly I was injured!' I said. 'It could have been fatal.'

'You have a remarkable ability to heal up very quickly.'

I said I had healed up, with over sixty pieces of metal, still embedded in my head. Plus the bits of cordite that kept coming out as blue spots.

'I've known people,' said the doctor, 'who have lost a complete ear and still acted.'

'I've never seen anybody in a film without an ear,' I said.

'Of course, you haven't. A temporary one has been put on by the make-up artist. I don't think you're going to get very much if you proceed with this case. I think you should settle out of court.'

'I haven't even had an offer yet.'

He said he would speak to the insurers. I managed to twitch a couple of times convulsively as he spoke, indicating that my nervous system was still in a state of shock. I went down to my car and climbed in. Just as I did so, he shouted down from a window. 'Ah hah, so you can still drive!'

I shut the door and wound my window down. 'Yes,' I shouted, 'but not terribly well.' Looking over my shoulder, I reversed into the car parked in the space 'reserved for the doctor'. Pretty rotten of me, I suppose, but the shouts of annoyance were well worth it.

'Sorry,' I said, 'motor region of the brain playing up a bit,' I made as much noise as I could as I roared away.

Shortly after that, came the call to attend the hospital for the plastic surgery. I packed a small bag and duly presented myself at a nursing home on the Lambeth Bridge Road. It appeared to be run by nuns. I arrived at seven and was due to be operated on by the same doctor who had pulled out the bits of metal at Stoke Mandeville. As I recall it was supposed to take place about ten o'clock. And I had been asked to eat nothing for the previous twenty-four hours.

I was put in the small waiting room. It was a cold winter's

day with snow drifting past the windows. It was even colder in the waiting room. I had been there about half an hour, reading the papers, when the door opened and a deranged person was wheeled in. I refrained from looking up from my papers as the deranged person issued a string of blood curdling threats, frequently banging himself on the head with his cane. This went on for at least fifteen minutes before a nun came in and removed him. I was then told by a nun to follow her, which I did, as she glided silently down the long corridor with a lot of religious motifs on the wall. I was shown into a room with an iron bedstead with a rubber mattress covered by a sheet and one blanket. I got into my pyjamas and lay down. Then I sat up and continued to read the papers. As there were no curtains to the windows, I decided I had better get dressed again, otherwise I was going to freeze to death before any operation could take place. I got dressed and climbed back into the bed and wished I had brought a hot-water bottle.

Near my bed on the wall there was a box with a red button on it. I assumed this was to summon assistance. Maybe they would have a hot-water bottle they could lend me. I pressed the button. To my surprise, this activated the hospital fire alarm system. An evacuation started to take place. Two or three nuns entered, almost simultaneously, and told me to get dressed.

'What's happening.' I said.

'Fire alarm,' they said.

'I'm afraid I did that,' I admitted. 'I thought it was sort of a bell for the nurses.'

The nuns disappeared to call off the evacuation. A senior nun arrived and told me sternly that I had caused considerable panic, and I mustn't do anything like that again. I apologized.

'Could I please have a hot-water bottle?'

'We don't supply hot-water bottles.'

'Oh really, why not?'

'Unfortunately, somebody had one that was very hot; they scalded themselves when it burst and tried to sue us.'

'I promise I won't sue you. I'm just freezing to death.'

'Very well, we'll see what we can do,' She reappeared with a stone hot-water bottle, which had an opening in the middle with a cork bung. The type very much favoured by Napoleon on his brief excursion to Russia. I thanked her profusely.

There was a small basin in the corner of the room and I tried to get the hole near the hot-water tap. I eventually rolled up my *Daily Mail* and made a tube to transport at least some into the receptacle. The tap ran slowly: in an effort to increase its volume, I managed to pull the handle off. A jet of hot water spouted in the air. I jammed the paper on it and pressed the bell again.

'We had to cut off the whole hot water system,' said a stern sister sometime later. 'You really are most troublesome.'

'I shouldn't be here at all.' I said. 'If I'd been Rex Harrison or that sort of actor, I'd be in Harley Street with an electric blanket!'

She produced a hypodermic and informed me that I was going to have a pre-op which would quieten me down. I took off my jacket and rolled up my sleeve. I was told to lower my trousers. I was getting it in the backside. And I should also be in my pyjamas. I lay there and started to feel drowsy. Even so, the thought of being operated on in this place did not appeal to me. If I had had a better part in the film, or indeed been Lionel Blair, I would have been in Harley Street. I wouldn't have been surprised if the companion in the anteroom had been the anaesthetist, and that the way he hit himself with his stick indicated that he would stop at nothing to make sure a patient was unconscious. I decided to leave.

I got out of bed and fell down. I crawled to the basin, and splashed cold water on my face – determined not to lose consciousness. Then I grabbed my overnight bag and, abandoning my pyjamas, which I only remembered later, headed for the door and staggered down the long corridor. A rather surprised sister saw me.

'You can't leave,' she said. 'The doctor's nearly ready to operate.'

'Bugger the doctor,' I said, 'I'm off.'

The sister clutched the hem of my long coat. I leaned forward at an angle of forty-five degrees and marched determinedly towards the end of the corridor and a short flight of stairs. Other nuns appeared. One shouted out: 'He's leaving; Oh Mother of God!'

'Stop him!' a voice from another corridor shouted: 'He can't leave, I'm about to operate.' This threat galvanized further efforts and after a short struggle with strong nuns I reached the glass-plated front door, and staggered into the blizzard that was now raging outside. Out of nowhere a taxi appeared with its light on. I staggered drunkenly as I waved it down.

'Blimey,' said the driver, 'you're on the sauce a bit early mate.'

I handed him a five-pound note and made him promise to take me to the Grafton Arms, even if I was unconscious when he arrived. I don't remember arriving at the Grafton Arms, but apparently Denis, who had a fruit barrow outside, said I stepped out looking fairly normal and said, 'If you see a nun, I'm not here,' and then fell down in the road. I woke up on the Major's sofa. I didn't open my eyes immediately, but I knew I was on the Major's sofa because I could hear a race commentary.

Happily, I did end up in the London Clinic. I believe even the anaesthetist was titled. My legal advisors added the cost to the bill. Judgement was given in my favour and I was awarded many thousands of pounds. All of which was swallowed up immediately in legal expenses. I had dinner with Charlotte, gave her the keys to the Lotus, which I still possessed, and took off for America.

6

At last I was going to work in Hollywood. I remember during the flight, looking back and thinking how remarkable that I should be heading that way. Although around the time I had met Jon Pertwee, I attended a dinner at which there had been a well-known seer into the future, who sat in a bedroom upstairs and for ten shillings told the dinner guests what was going to happen to them. I had been told I was going to be able to give up selling paint and would become a writer. None of which I had taken too much notice of at the time, but which had indeed come to pass. She also mentioned that I would be an actor. True again. And I still had the scars to prove it. She also said that I would go to America and here I was on my way there. Unfortunately, she also told me that I would die around about the age of sixty in my pyjamas – or was it the Bahamas? I couldn't remember too clearly. I made a mental note that around that age, to avoid the Bahamas, and I would certainly give up wearing pyjamas at about fifty-five, which I did. Come to think of it, it could have been eating bananas. That is a rather worrying thought, as I had one this morning. I am rather glad I am writing this – these warnings tend to slip easily from one's mind.

*   *   *

While I make this plane journey, I might as well recount another accident that stands out in my mind. Once again it occurred whilst I was playing the part of a twit in a film called *Just For Fun!* This time it was as the son of the Prime Minister. I found myself on the film set at Pinewood Studios, having completed what I thought was my final scene in the film. The only scene left to shoot was that in which the son of the Prime Minister gets into a diving suit and is lowered from a boat into the Atlantic. Arriving at the bottom, he takes out an axe and chops through the London to New York telephone cable to prevent the news of some shady share deal being found out. A typical, highbrow British film plot. *The Times* was right, I did do some 'B' movies.

'I wonder,' I said to the director, 'how you're going to take the underwater bit?' I was told a man from the diving school was already there; my suit awaited me.

'Good heavens,' I said. 'I can't possibly get into a diving suit. I've got claustrophobia. Surely you've got a stunt man?'

'We haven't,' said the director, 'and this is no time to have claustrophobia. It's practically four o'clock and I'm hoping to get this in the can today. Special effects have got the tank ready; we're running short of time, so get a move on.'

I was taken into a room where there was a diving instructor and an old-fashioned diving suit; the sort I had seen John Wayne wearing once in a film when he fought an octopus. It had a copper helmet and lead boots, which appeared to be separated from each other by about eight feet of rubber diving suit. 'It's a bit big,' I said.

'It concertinas up when you put it on,' said the instructor, a small bald man who seemed permanently short of breath. I was stripped down to my underwear. My wrists and ankles were covered in French chalk and I was eased into the suit. I sat on a chair as the heavy collar was put on, then the lead boots. I stood up. I swayed about. I found I could lean at quite an acute angle without falling down. The boots were so heavy, I couldn't lift a foot.

'Perfick fit,' said the instructor. He and his assistant took my arms and dragged me to the set, where there was part of a big boat in a large tank of water, in which also floated a rowing boat. A crane lifted me into the air and deposited me in the rowing boat.

'Now come the lead weights,' said the man from the diving school. His assistant produced a large lead weight which he hung on my chest, then one on my back. The result was the seat broke and had to be replaced by a box.

'Do I have to do this?' I asked.

'Come on!' said the director. 'We haven't got much time. There's a ladder down the side of the boat. You've got to climb out, go down the ladder and disappear.'

'What?! Underwater?!'

'Yes, of course.'

'What about my claustrophobia?'

'Noffink to worry about,' said the man from the diving school.

'It's only forty feet deep; there's a camera down there to record everything you do.'

'Everything I do,' I said, 'is getting an axe and cutting through a piece of cable. It's not really very much. I mean anybody can do that. Apart from which you won't see a lot of me, with that helmet on. You'll only see my nose.'

'In that case,' said the director, 'wave your nose about a lot, so we'll know it's you.'

The helmet was put over my head and clicked into place. Fortunately the little round door at the front was still open. I peered out anxiously; didn't I need some instruction from the experts on what to do?

'Keep breathing is the main thing,' said the man from the diving school.

'Yes, I'll do that,' I said. 'Look I've got very low blood pressure; it's not going to be affected by the weight of the water, is it?'

The director lit his fortieth cigarette and said he couldn't stand temperamental actors.

'Now,' said the man from the diving school, 'I'll explain exactly what 'appens. So pay attention! The tube from this 'ere 'elmet goes to that piece of equipment on the deck of that big boat. On the deck of that boat is my assistant, who is going to turn the 'andle on the side of that machine, which 'as got a device on it, which will pump air into the 'elmet on your 'ead, and you will breathe that air when it arrives. This equipment 'as given satisfactory service since it was made. I've even been down in it myself.'

'It's dangerous?' I said.

'Well divers have been known to fall off their ropes and 'ead for the bottom, and if it's deep enough they get what we call in the trade a blood orange.'

'Good heavens,' I said, 'that sounds ghastly. What's that?'

'Your whole body is forced into your 'elmet. But that won't 'appen to you. You've got to be in the Atlantic or somewhere deep for that to happen. This will be a piece of cake.'

It was too late to resign from the film, but I must admit to a feeling of slight apprehension as the man from the diving school placed his hand on the small door that separated me from the outside world.

'Now,' he said, 'I'm going to shut the door and lock it. My mate will start winding the 'andle; and the air will arrive and you will breathe it in. Should you 'ave any problems, you will give the correct diver's signal, which means I 'ave a problem.'

'What is the correct signal?' I said.

'You will clench your fist and bang your 'elmet.'

I clenched my fist in readiness; he shut the door. I waited for what seemed like an eternity. Finally, I heard the rush of air on its way. It sounded rather like a tube train arriving at Piccadilly Circus from a long distance. It arrived and I took a deep breath, but it seemed to pass me by. I don't know where it went, but it certainly didn't go up my nose. I rapped on my helmet with my clenched fist. The director opened the door.

RIGHT: *My father making a rare appearance, together with grandma and my first wife, Dawn, attending the film premiere of* We Joined The Navy.

A small me on a beach with my mother who had wonderful teeth.

RIGHT: *Twenty-nine and unaware that one day I'd own quite a few of these cars that I could actually drive.*

ABOVE: *My first film and I'm back at school in* School for Scoundrels.

RIGHT: *A bowler-hatted twit in the* Billy Cotton Show!

ABOVE RIGHT: *My first big part. A p.o.w. in* A Very Important Person.

FAR RIGHT: We Joined The Navy – *and I get a rollicking from Lloyd Nolan. Kenneth More is hoping I'll remember my lines.*

ABOVE: *With Charlie – what a smasher.*

ABOVE RIGHT: *A hippy theatrical agent in* Smashing Time. *Lynn Redgrave is clearly thrilled to be acting with me.*

LEFT: *In* Robert & Elizabeth *I had built-up boots, making me 6'7". Dear Angela Richards had to stand on her toes for our love song.*

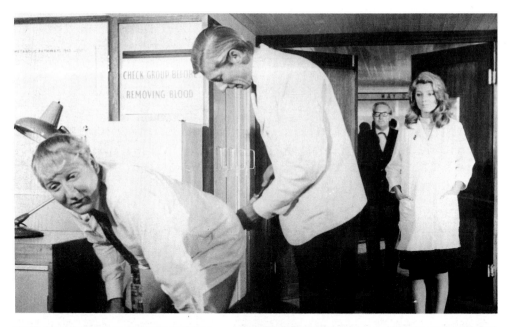

LEFT: *Giving Leslie Phillips a youth injection in* Doctor in Clover. *No wonder he looks worried, this is take fourteen.*

BELOW LEFT: *Forty years old, a Rolls and Joanna Lumley. All I needed now was a haircut.*

BELOW FAR LEFT: *Dancing in the party scene in* Laugh In. *Much practice in night clubs pays off at last.*

RIGHT: *The original cast of* Are You Being Served?

BELOW: *The cast of* 'Allo 'Allo *already practising for a united Europe.*

*Captain Beaky is the best thing
I've ever done and the most fun.*

RIGHT: *With my wife, Collette.
Yes, she does look small to be a
liontamer.*

'Any problems?'

'Yes,' I said. 'That air missed me completely. It went straight by. It's probably down somewhere near by left leg; it didn't stay long enough in my helmet to have a go at it.'

'Could be a leak,' said the man from the diving school. 'We'll put a 'andle on the other end, and we'll both give it a go.'

A handle was placed on the other end of the ancient bellows-type piece of equipment. Once again the door was shut, and I clenched my fist. The handles were turned at great speed. It was as though ten tube trains had arrived at once; I had more air than I could cope with. My lead boots flew off; my arms sprang out and I suddenly took on the appearance of the Michelin Man, as air escaped from my wrists and ankles to the accompaniment of loud raspberries. I couldn't bend an arm to knock on my helmet, but my predicament was obvious. The director unscrewed the little door at the front of my helmet and I fizzed back to normal size.

'I don't know how such a simple scene can take so long,' said the director, lighting another cigarette. 'We're going to have to go on overtime.'

'Does that include me,' I said.

'No, you're on a flat fee so don't keep causing trouble.'

'I'm doing my very best,' I said, 'to be a diver. I didn't realize I was employed to do my own stunts. I'm not sure Equity would approve.'

My boots were replaced and everything was set to go again. Then the director had an inspiration.

'Look!' he said. 'You, as the Prime Minister's son, are playing an idiot, right?'

'Right,' I said. 'In fact, I think I'm a complete idiot to be in this film at all.'

It was clear that tempers were getting frayed.

'Calm down,' said the director. 'I've just had a wonderful idea.' And taking another cigarette, he lit it, and placed it between my lips.

'This is the gag: we shut the door and you're lifted into the air. Just as you're being dropped into the sea, you tap on your helmet.'

'The sign that suggests something's seriously wrong?' The instructor gave me the thumbs up!

'You're lifted back and your father, the Prime Minister, opens the door and finds you smoking a cigarette. This will get a big laugh.' The director gave a loud laugh to indicate how well this 'gag' would go.

I had been writing quite a lot of comedy up till then and I failed to see how it would get a big laugh. Unless my father, the Prime Minister, said something. So I suggested he should say: 'How could I have a son that is such an idiot?' It wasn't really funny, but at least it would have given him something to say as he removed the cigarette. Unluckily, it appeared that the Prime Minister had got bored waiting and had gone home. I held the cigarette between my lips, the little door was shut. Unfortunately it was rather a long cigarette. And the door was rather near to my nose. The cigarette immediately tilted up and connected its glowing end to the aforementioned nose, I was hauled in the air, banging furiously on my helmet to indicate that something had gone seriously wrong. I was pulled back and dropped down. A hand purporting to be that of the Prime Minister opened the little door; the cigarette remained fixed to my nose.

The director pulled it off. 'This is not my day,' he said. He called for make-up to repair the damage. Finally with only a few minutes to spare, I was lowered beneath the water. I clung onto the ladder and started climbing down. It seemed endless. Angling my head, I could get one eye level with the little window. I looked for the camera. I couldn't see it. But I could feel water coming in the suit. Mainly around the collar and the crutch. I hurriedly climbed up the ladder again. I seemed to be getting heavier as I did so. My head appeared in the lights; I rapped desperately on my helmet, which by now was filling up with water. The director opened the door, some water came out.

'I'm leaking,' I said.

'My God!' said the director, 'this certainly isn't my day. Tomorrow we'll get a stunt man.'

From then on I decided that doing my own stunts was not a frightfully good idea. The only other accident which was really quite hilarious at the time and didn't harm anybody, except perhaps the nerves of the stage manager, was whilst I was on stage in *Robert and Elizabeth*, dressed in my Life Guards kit. I got my spurs locked together as I bade Elizabeth Moulton Barrett farewell in her tiny Victorian bedroom as she lay supposedly dying. She weakly waved a hand, I clicked my heels together and to my horror found that my spurs had locked behind me. I tried to move and started to tilt dangerously forward, holding my helmet under my arm. I crashed down with my breast plate and helmet, all six feet seven or eight of me in by built-up boots. The invalid's bed collapsed and a strong Australian voice, which was her normal voice, said:

'Strewth, I think he's broken my leg.'

I hadn't, of course. But as I stood up, my breast plate fell off and my helmet rolled into the orchestra pit and, very red-faced, I retired to howls of laughter from the audience.

I don't want any would-be film-makers to read this and think I was a liability. I am just condensing one or two accidents together while I fly to Los Angeles to join Harold Robbins for the next adventure.

I arrived at the Beverly Hills Hotel on my first trip to that side of America. Hollywood is known as the Coast, because the sea is only about forty-five minutes away at Malibu. Property prices are high and it is a very smart place to live. Years later, I became a regular visitor.

At first glance, the Beverly Hills Hotel looks like a cake with pink icing on it, surrounded by tall green palm trees, and behind which are extensive gardens, tennis courts, and a swimming pool. Everybody who was anybody in those days used to meet there in the Polo Lounge. I wasn't anybody, but this didn't stop me sitting in the Polo Lounge, spotting famous faces. I remember meeting a small elderly man wearing a sweat shirt with the words: 'I love Jackie Oakie' (an actor I remember playing Mussolini in *The Great Dictator*) on it. I asked him if he had ever met the prominent actor. He told me he *was* Jackie Oakie. I retreated, embarrassed.

Harold introduced me to the author of the book I was to work on, about the mean old recluse. The author was a middle-aged, nice enough chap, but didn't have a great sense of humour. In fact he was one of those rare people that leave you wanting less, which is why I suppose I had been invited to write with him. I can't say it was a very enjoyable experience. I found myself locked in the luxury of the hotel, arguing a lot, and felt very lonely. I knew nobody, and rarely saw Harold, who was busy on a number of other projects. I remember writing to Charlotte, saying what a lousy place Hollywood was, and if ever I enjoyed Hollywood, I must have lost my soul! I didn't know that in a few year's time I would be enjoying Hollywood thoroughly, writing and acting in *Rowan & Martin's Laugh In* and losing my soul all over the place. But at this time, I felt lonely and insecure.

Charlotte wrote back saying her acting career was going well, and she was going to Switzerland for a holiday in a couple of weeks. She gave me an address to write to. I persevered with the collaboration, but in the end decided I couldn't take Hollywood any more, and told Harold I was leaving. He told me I was an idiot. Nevertheless, he still believed that one day I would be a successful writer. I packed my bag and was just leaving the hotel, when a familiar voice said, 'Jeremy Lloyd! Good Lord! What are you doing here?' I turned round and found myself face to face with Eve Arden in whose show I had appeared some years before. She said I needed a holiday and packed me into her shooting brake, and drove me to a lovely ranch house in Hidden Valley, where she and her husband Brooks lived an idyllic existence. They were two of the kindest people I have ever met. I stayed there for a week:

riding, eating well and finally recuperating enough to fly back to London.

Remembering that Charlotte was still in Switzerland, I grabbed a suitcase and took off. I flew to Zurich and got a taxi. Half-way up a mountain, the driver told me that due to an avalanche he couldn't go any further. 'The village you want is down there.'

It was nearly dark, but I could see some lights twinkling a long way below me. I paid him off, grabbed my suitcase and tobogganed down the icy slope. I was soaking wet by the time I made the village and half-frozen. I made my way to the address, only to find that Charlotte had left the day before. I decided to find an hotel.

As I walked through the village, I spotted her, arm in arm, with a rather good-looking ski instructor. She didn't see me, so I hid behind the pump in the centre of the village and popped out at the last minute saying, 'Hello, how are you?' She was very surprised, and assured me I was the only person she knew who would pop out from behind a pump in the middle of a remote village somewhere in Switzerland at eight o'clock in the evening. She did have a great sense of humour, but it appeared that the ski instructor, although handsome, didn't.

She had moved into a small hotel, where I joined her. The next day we caught a train to Zermatt and stayed there for three weeks. She was a marvellous skier; I was rotten. In fact, I was banned from skiing after accidentally going down a black run. I remember sitting on my haunches, with my sticks held straight out shouting: '*Achtung! Achtung!*' This is a normal warning given when skiers are out of control. I crashed through the side of a flimsy hut at the bottom and had to be thawed out. I was reported for dangerous skiing, and spent the rest of the holiday admiring Charlotte through binoculars, as she disappeared up and down the slopes, on her own or accompanied by some bronze god. She was always very popular.

By 1967 I had rented a cottage in Kensington and continued writing sporadically at the Grafton Arms. I appeared in quite a good movie with Lynn Redgrave and Rita Tushingham, called *Smashing Time*. I played a hippy. Actually I did look rather like a hippy in those days. I had long hair, wore a lot of chains and beads, and boots with Cuban heels. I turned up like that once at my father's place, driving an Italian racing car called an Iso Grifo. He really thought I'd gone to the dogs. Particularly when I told him how much the car had cost. I think it was the equivalent of about £50,000 today. By then, he was confined to a wheel chair; apparently as the result of a stroke. Although I didn't know it at the time, he *hadn't* had a stroke, but got into the wheel chair, when anybody arrived. It was terribly sad, but I suppose it was an excuse for not having much to do.

The Iso Grifo could often be seen parked outside Alvaro's famous restaurant on the King's Road at lunchtime on Saturdays. This was the 'in' place to be. Everybody who was anybody met there for Saturday lunch. I managed to be in Hollywood and had hardly met anybody; here I became friendly with Sammy Davis Jr, Peter Lawford, and Ryan O'Neal – there seemed to be a lot of American actors in London in those days. I even met Woody Allen, who is one of my idols. I think having such an attractive fiancée as Charlotte might have helped. They were certainly all very keen to meet her. Years later of course, she starred with Woody Allen in *Stardust Memories*.

'Flower power' was in full swing in London: shops like Carrot on Wheels were selling see through crochet mini dresses to the girls, whilst I was trying to get used to those Cuban boots and, at thirty-seven, was wondering whether to have a face lift or not, to keep up with the excitement. But I didn't. Charlotte had lost a stone out of her engagement ring, which of course was an omen. And one day her father called round to see me to say she didn't think she could go through with the marriage. That was rather unfortunate as the banns had already been called twice, and the invitations were on their way. I think her family was as upset as I was. But we did manage to have one last happy summer at St Tropez before we finally parted. She gave me a lovely Kchinsky watch with 'Time in my heart forever' engraved on the back. I had it for years before it was stolen in a French hotel. Fortunately our friendship is still intact and I still get Christmas cards from her.

To cheer me up after parting with Charlotte, I was invited to stay for a couple of weeks in Jamaica by two splendid sisters called Penny and Ginny Rhodes. They had a lovely house called the Bird Cage, which overlooked the sea in Ocho Rios. I can only describe them as real tomboys and game for adventure; they assured me I hadn't lived unless I had shot the rapids on Dunn's River, famous for it's cascading falls. We weren't actually going to shoot the falls, but apparently the rapids were very good. So we drove to Port Antonio to begin our journey. I assumed it wouldn't be particularly hazardous, so I took my guitar along, and they took picnic baskets. We went down to the water's edge to find a raftman who would take us on board. There were about twelve raftmen waiting with their rafts; each one leaning on his pole. They were all smoking very large badly rolled cigarettes and looked what I can only describe as very relaxed. The rafts were very primitive affairs: each had a bench seat, with a basketwork chair nailed to it. We chose three raftmen who looked as though they could actually make the journey and climbed aboard our respective craft.

'Is this dangerous?' I enquired.

'It's a piece of cake, man,' said the raftman, inhaling deeply. I helped him on board. With a lithe movement he poled us away from the bank and, with the others following, we were off on our journey. The river was quite slow-running at the beginning and we passed through idyllic tropical scenery. The only living soul I remember seeing was a native washing clothes in the river and banging them with a stone. Next to her was the largest box of Daz I had ever seen. I was in the middle of a calypso, trying to think of a rhyme for rapids, when we arrived at them. I remember it was quite an exciting experience as I clung on. I realize now why the raftman had a big joint before he started; he was even more relaxed about the whole thing, as we plunged into the foaming waters. If you haven't done this journey, I can thoroughly recommend it.

'That was a little one,' the raftman said. 'We get to the big stuff, man, further on.'

The girls, of course, were screaming with delight. I tried to think of something that rhymed with 'rotten swimmer'. I had just decided on 'home for dinner', when we shot a number of rapids, one after the other. By now we were all begging the raftmen for a puff of ganja to calm our nerves. After about half an hour of hair raising excitement, we rounded a bend and reached a placid part of the river where we moored under some trees, for a swim and to have the picnic. I must say, Jamaica is a very beautiful place, particularly after the raftmen had passed round the local habit for a puff. By the time we had set off again, I had insisted on taking the pole, while the raftman slept in my chair. I attacked the next lot of rapids with relish, shouting over my shoulder, 'Move it, man!' to one of the following rafts. Finally, we arrived at Port Antonio just as darkness fell. Somehow I had managed to lose my guitar on the trip. I don't remember where. We waited for a while in case it floated down, but I never saw it again. We were driven in a sort of armoured vehicle, back up river, to collect our little mini moke.

At that time there were a lot of troubles in Jamaica, and I remember stones being thrown and sticks banging on the side of the vehicle as we drove through the villages. In those days it was not a good idea to break down, unless you were outside a police station. One night we went to a place called The Yellow Banana Hat Nightclub, which was, to say the least, rather off the beaten track. The music was great and I was wiping my brow after strutting my stuff on the floor with the girls when a very large man approached me and pulled out a tape measure. He went through a mime routine of measuring me up. I had a sudden sinking feeling that he might be the local undertaker and knew something that I didn't. I was quite relieved when he said he was going to make me a suit.

'I don't actually want a suit,' I said.

'You'll like this suit, man. It'll be the best suit you've ever had.'

'That's very kind,' I said. 'But I'm actually not in need of a suit at the moment.'

'This is not just any suit,' he assured me. 'This suit will have very wide shoulders; they will be out here.' He indicated this was the sort of suit that would fit Arnold Schwarzenegger.

I shook my head. By now quite a crowd had gathered round.

'I'm telling you, man. This suit is very special.'

'What's so special?' I enquired.

'It is special, man, because when you get home you can smoke the shoulders.' The crowd roared with laughter and I had a mental picture of me walking through Immigration at Heathrow Airport with my shoulders full of ganja, explaining that I had no idea how it got there.

By the time we had done the limbo and drunk the local beer, it was about three o'clock in the morning. We jumped into the mini moke and headed back towards the Bird Cage. I suppose we were about eight miles from home when there was a sudden crash as something hit the back of the moke. I looked over my shoulder and saw three grinning faces on the front bench seat of an old Cadillac; three sets of white teeth grinned from under the brims of three large hats.

'Good heavens!' said Penny. 'It's the Kingston Boys. They're a jolly rough crowd.' The Cadillac rammed us again. I kept the accelerator firmly on the floor as my heart sank. The Cadillac pulled out, accelerated, and eased up alongside.

'You've got a lot of action in there, man,' the nearest hat informed me.

'These are trainee nuns,' I shouted. 'And I'm Father O'Flannigan. God bless you, boys.'

The driver leant across and shouted: 'Hey, don't you want to share that great looking pussy?'

Before I could discuss the unlikeliness of this event, a corner had arrived. I had seen it, but the Cadillac driver hadn't. He went straight on and disappeared into the jungle. I kept my foot firmly on the floor as we broadsided round the corner.

'I don't think they mean any harm,' said Ginny. 'They're just out for a bit of fun.'

'Out for a bit of fun?' I said. 'If he hadn't missed the corner, you could have found yourself in deep trouble. God knows what would have happened to me.'

We nearly got back to the Bird Cage when the headlights of the Cadillac once again appeared in my mirror. Now I must explain that the Bird Cage was on a private estate. At the entrance of the estate, there was a guard with a gun. In those troubled times, most of the estates had this sort of arrangement. The Cadillac lights were suddenly switched on full beam and once again it crashed into the back of the moke.

'They're very keen on you,' I said. 'It's a pity you're so attractive. It's proving to be quite a drawback.'

The girls turned round and gave our pursuers the V-sign; it's amazing how brave girls are in these situations. I did consider slowing down and throwing them out, but they were actually both stronger than me. So I decided against it. There was one last sweeping bend to negotiate before the entrance to the estate and I took it flat out. The Cadillac suspension couldn't quite cope with it. It started to slide sideways as the driver wrestled wildly with the wheel, and the last I saw of it in my mirror were the headlights pointing at the sky as the back end fell down into a ditch. I kept my hand pressed on the horn as I approached the guard gate, but even this and my shout as I passed failed to wake the guard who was fast asleep by his hut.

I must say I was glad to get back to the safety of the Bird Cage. We locked the door and retired to bed. I had a room downstairs and the girls slept upstairs in a room with a balcony. Slightly shaken from my adventure, I decided I probably couldn't sleep and picked up a magazine and started to read with interest the story of the Charge of the Light Brigade. I was in the middle of associating myself with Lord Cardigan's reckless charge at the rushing guns, when there was a creak at my door, which led directly to the patio outside. To my horror I saw the handle turning. Fortunately I had locked the door. If my hair could have stood up on end, I am sure it would have done so. I heard some heavy breathing, and then footsteps disappearing. I thought the would-be intruder had gone away, but in fact, he had walked round to the back of the house and climbed up the trellis work onto the balcony, waking Penny the younger sister, who was at least six feet three in high heels. And although she wasn't wearing them, she was still a formidable sight, no doubt, as she rose from her bed, marched onto the balcony and punched the would-be intruder, square between the eyes. He fell back with a wild shout and severely damaged himself on the concrete path. I don't know whether it was one of the Kingston Boys, but whoever it was, he was last seen hobbling off into the distance, using very colourful language.

I hope this won't put anybody off going to Jamaica for their holidays. All this happened well over twenty years ago, when life was a bit more exciting. And I can thoroughly recommend the sports there. By this I don't mean the Rhodes, sisters. But the deep-sea fishing is great fun; the only sad thing is when you catch a fish. The sight of a blue shining tuna or sail fish leaping out of the water on the end of your line, as you strain to reel it in, is quite something. But I am afraid I couldn't take it when the boatman actually killed the fish. I wanted to let it go. The one I caught would have certainly fed quite a large family, which is where I am sure it ended up. Fishing for freshwater shrimp is also quite exciting. As you get your net down on the bed of the stream the shrimp manage to propel themselves about three feet out of the water to escape being caught. It is quite a sight, particularly when you hit a shoal of them. They are like underwater crickets. And fried up make a great meal. I will always remember the wonderful sunsets and fireflies on a black velvet night; the amazing electrical storms and the almost endless sunshine. I must say it was one of the best holidays I have ever had. I know that, because I was quite sorry to come home. And normally I am very relieved to be leaving somewhere. I am not a very good holiday person.

I remember once going to Africa to recover from a very bad bout of flu. My doctor had recommended a hotel in Mombasa, and I arrived at about two o'clock in the afternoon in what I can only describe as sweltering heat. As I stepped through the front door, the voice on the tannoy announced that there would be bingo at eight o'clock. I am not a snob, but I didn't think a bingo evening was quite what I was looking for. I checked into my room, which I thought was very average, opened the sliding doors and stepped straight out onto the beach.

It was about 120 degrees Fahrenheit and the white sand stretched ahead of me. I was wearing a pair of denim trousers, a shirt and a pair of sneakers. I strolled across the beach, sweat pouring off me, and walked straight into the sea. I floated around for a bit and then started to march back up the beach, which was on a slight incline. The current had caused me to drift someway way past the hotel; it seemed quite a long walk back along the beach. I suddenly began to get giddy. I saw a small clump of trees and headed for them, lay down and passed out. I woke up to find a black bird with what seemed to be about a forty-foot wingspan, circling above me, and looking down interestedly. It was joined by another bird. They obviously thought I was a body washed up after a shipwreck. I was rather pale and thin at the time. I struggled to my feet and hurriedly returned to my room. Picking up the phone, I enquired what time the next plane left. I was told if I hurried there was one at six o'clock. I was on it. But it wasn't actually going to London, it was going to Bombay. I didn't care. I had seen enough of Africa that afternoon to last me a long time.

After a cup of tea in Bombay, I caught a connecting flight to London. The next day I was walking down the King's Road in Chelsea and I was stopped by a friend who said, 'When are you actually going to Africa?'

'I went yesterday,' I said. 'It was great fun.'

I think it was then that I decided that if I couldn't have a decent holiday in a first class hotel, I would rather not go at all. Unless of course I happened to be going to Barbados; almost any hotel there is good. It is certainly one of the prettiest islands in the Caribbean: peaceful and nobody tries to sell you suits with large shoulders.

7

In 1971 I went on tour with a play called *The Avengers*. This, of course, was the stage version of the popular television series in which I had already made one or two appearances. But in the play I was cast as an MI5 twit. The play was very ably directed by Leslie Phillips, who was a friend of mine – well, certainly before the rehearsals started. It starred Simon Oates, Sue Lloyd and Kate O'Mara. I was assured my billing wouldn't be smaller than half of anybody else's and as soon as I saw the first publicity poster, I got a tape measure out to make sure that indeed I was the right size. I was about an eighth of an inch under. I complained to the producer, who assured me it wouldn't make any difference to my performance. It is funny. As a writer, I get very fed up with temperamental actors; as an actor, I immediately feel temperamental. That is perhaps the reason I can understand actors so well when I am writing for them.

I had temporary rooms above a garage in a mews apartment owned by Sue Lloyd. Her other paying guest was Kate O'Mara, so it was a handy set-up to rehearse our parts. At that time I was worried about the onset of age and had been to Paris to obtain a youth-giving extract, manufactured in Switzerland, sold in Paris and banned in England. These phials of life preservative had to be kept at a very low temperature and I remember travelling from Paris to the mews with them in a portable deepfreeze where they were duly placed in Sue Lloyd's fridge.

We rehearsed in London and then proceeded to Birmingham for an opening night in Sue Lloyd's ancient Rolls. It was decided upon arriving at the digs in Hagley Road that it would be cheaper if we all shared the same bedroom. Just actors saving money. Sue, who is a diabetic, is an expert injector, as she is used to giving herself a shot when needed. I remember clinging onto the mantelpiece as she pulled down my pyjamas and gave me a quick shot in the bottom of my youth drug, while Kate O'Mara buried her head in a pillow having hysterics. I must say that was probably the jolliest time of the whole tour.

The Avengers on stage was quite an ambitious production: there was even a Bentley for Steed to drive onto the stage – it was made of wood, but looked very realistic. The rehearsals went on late into the night, every night – Leslie Phillips being a perfectionist. Apparently, in the course of the play, I had somehow become hypnotized and managed to repeat passages of everybody's previous speeches, which was rather a confusing thing for an actor to do, as I really didn't have any key lines to get my cues from. I would suddenly just burst into a flood of incoherent nonsense.

Well, it was finally judged that the play was ready to receive an audience, and on the opening night we all gathered nervously, hoping the special effects would work, not to mention the fact that we hoped we would all remember our dialogue – particularly me. I was very nervous on these occasions. Not being a professional stage actor, it was very nerve-wracking and I was sick in the dressing room before I went down and stood in the wings for half an hour, before I got my cue to go on.

The play had some very complicated technology. Kate O'Mara played a sort of mysterious Madame X, who could disappear at various times and would have been a credit to Paul Daniels. One of her disappearing acts was on a revolving sofa: she would press a button and the sofa would revolve just as she opened an umbrella. And when the umbrella shut, she was gone. I hadn't taken particular notice of how this effect worked, but I was very impressed that it did. The play opened with an unfortunate accident in which the Bentley which Steed was supposed to drive on had to be pushed on. But as it was pushed on, the front wheel fell off, rolled across the stage and bounced down into the first row. This got a smattering of applause. Then came a long scene in which I had to recline on the sofa, talking a lot of nonsense and hopefully getting some laughs. I was rather nervous and perhaps not being the tidiest actor in the world I was waving my arms about and accidentally pressed the secret button. This, I might add, was before Kate O'Mara had used it herself – as she was to disappear in a later scene. The seat of the sofa immediately revolved, taking my whole body with it, except for my head and my left foot, which remained in view. Inextricably trapped, I continued with my dialogue, and the audience went into hysteria. Two scene hands had to come on and physically remove the sofa, while I still spoke my lines. It was rather a good exit I thought, and rather a hard act to follow.

Poor Sue had to wear a sort of rubber frogman's suit and appear out of a helicopter, which was lowered onto the stage. This suit made her so hot that she used to faint in the wings and had to be revived with a Coca-Cola, the sugar content bringing her back to consciousness. I must say all in all, acting on stage really does get the adrenalin going when things go wrong.

In another scene I was supposed to be shot in the arm and somebody from wardrobe was waiting in the wings with a bloodstained sling, which I would don and appear for another scene. Unfortunately the actor who was supposed to shoot me after he had been hit on the head, fell to his knees wildly pulling the trigger, and the gun failed to go off. As he reached floor level, the gun did go off, but by then it was pointing at my knee. I clutched my knee and hopped off stage. I donned the bloodstained sling. On cue, I returned to answer the question, 'And what happened to you?' I replied that I had been shot in the leg, fallen down and broken my arm. These brilliant moments of improvization always get a good laugh from an audience.

We did finally make it to London with the play, but unfortunately it went the way of so many ingenious productions. I read a review that said: 'This man Jeremy Lloyd is a great find, perhaps a new Leslie Phillips.' I did assure Leslie his mantle had not been stirred or even slightly shaken. After all it was only a local paper in Billingham. I wish I had kept some of those reviews.

I did quite a few films in those days, usually playing the upper class twit that I perfected on the *Billy Cotton Show.* Actually I had perfected it long before that – I think probably when I was a paint salesman. One of my better parts was in the film *Doctor in Clover* with James Robertson Justice, Leslie Phillips and Shirley Ann Field. It was made at Pinewood and was great fun. Casting in those days was often at the White Elephant in Curzon Street. I used to pop in there quite often for a cheap lunch, like an omelette, knowing that film producers frequented the place. It was during one of these omelettes that the producer of *Doctor in Clover* said, 'Oh hello, Jeremy. We're doing a doctor film, would you like to be in it?'

It was as easy as that. Unfortunately I don't think it is quite as easy today. Although, in life, I still think you have got to be in the right place at the right time. Five minutes late isn't good enough. I think I only did *Desert Island Discs* for Michael Parkinson because I happened to bump into him on a beach one day. He had just taken over the show and still hadn't filled up his guest list. I managed to relate some of my more harrowing adventures of my earlier life on it and, as a result, received a number of letters from caring ladies who offered to look after me. As you can see in this extended version of my not uneventful time on planet earth, I have probably been quite lucky in the 'being looked after' stakes.

I appeared in a film called *Man in the Moon* which starred Kenneth More and also Shirley Ann Field once more. In it I was merely playing a motorist, who had to drive an XK140, drop-head, full speed down a country lane, round a corner and pick up Shirley Ann, who was hitch-hiking. The director called for the XK140 to be driven up and asked me if I felt confident that I could handle this car and drive as quickly as possible into view, giving the impression of a dare devil sort of chap. I told him I was rather keen on cars and would do my best to oblige.

'Can I try it our first?' I asked.

'Certainly,' said the director.

I jumped in, revved up, banged into first, whipped through the gears and disappeared round the corner in a cloud of dust. I was away for about an hour, trying it out and managed to get it moving fairly quickly, I thought. I then returned to say I was ready for the stunt. The director was furious: I was only supposed to have tried it out for five minutes, just to make sure I could get it moving down the road.

'Right,' he said. 'There's a camera crew stationed on this corner; they will film you coming rapidly down this country lane; you will then brake for the corner; make the tyres squeal a bit and if you can't, we'll put that on after as special effects. You will see Miss Field, you will stop, pick her up, stop again and do your dialogue and she'll slap your face. Is that clear?'

'Yes,' I said.

'We'd better rehearse the face slapping,' said the director.

'Lean out of the car.' I leant out. 'Shirley,' said the director, 'slap Jeremy on the face.'

'Certainly,' said Shirley. Swinging her arm back, she gave me quite a good slap across the chops.

'That was lousy,' said the director. 'Don't you know how to slap someone?' He took back his hand, which I noticed was the size of a small spade, whacked it across my jaw and I fell unconscious between the seats. When I came round, he apologized, saying I must have a glass chin.

'Quite all right, Basil,' I said. 'I'm sure it's all part of the job.' Still slightly dizzy, I revved up the car, disappeared again in a cloud of smoke and waited about half a mile away for my cue – there being a series of signals between me and the corner where the camera crew were waiting. I got the cue.

'Right, I'll show them I can drive really quickly,' I said to myself. I went off with a wheel spin, approached the corners pretty quickly, slammed on the anchors, lost the back end, wrestled wildly with the wheel, managed to stay on the road and finally pulled up next to Shirley Ann Field. I thought she looked very pale.

'Hello,' I said. 'Like a lift?' She burst out laughing. I looked round. The camera crew were a few hundred yards away, having retreated at the corner, assuming they were in imminent danger. The director was not too pleased.

'Are you mad?' he said. 'Are you trying to kill us all?'

'No, Basil,' I said. 'I was just coming round the corner quickly as ordered.'

'Go back down the road and do it again.'

'Yes, Basil.'

I went back down the road and did it again. I came round the corners very slowly, stopped and said, 'Hello. Would you like a lift?'

Shirley got in. I drove a little way down the road, then she got out, leant forward and whacked me on the side of the face; it was quite a good whack actually and I saw stars for a moment. But I managed to shut the door, give her a salute and drive off.

'Cut!' shouted Basil. 'We'll do that again.'

We did *that* again about twenty times. The left side of my face was considerably larger than the right by the time we had done it to the director's satisfaction. I don't think Basil liked me; I didn't particularly like Basil. But I did like Shirley and I drove her home after filming and we both had a good laugh about it. Though I could only laugh on one side of my face.

Returning to the Grafton Arms and the seemingly normal world, I got to work on yet another *Dickie Henderson Special*. The phone rang and the gallant Major, who was on the other line talking to his bookies, motioned me to pick it up. I picked it up and found myself talking to a man called George Slaughter. George is America's answer to Billy Connolly, though I am sure Billy Connolly was in his pram at this time, as this was in 1969. He was the producer of the popular American show called *Rowan & Martin's Laugh In*.

Had the Grafton organization any talent they could offer to write in America?

'Yes,' I said. 'They've got Jeremy Lloyd. He's our best writer. He's written for Harold Robbins. He writes for the top comedy shows here. He's expensive, but he's good. In fact, he's the best we've got.'

'Could he be at the Dorchester Hotel tomorrow about eight o'clock in the morning?' Mr Slaughter enquired.

'He could,' I assured him. I put the phone down. Major Grafton enquired who I had been talking to. I told him.

'You can't go,' he said. 'We need you here.'

I assured him that I was at least going for the interview. He pointed out that if I got the job, I would have to pay him ten per cent commission as he was also my agent. I pointed out that I had answered the phone, while he was busy with his bookie. It was an awkward moment. Finally, I gave in and agreed.

George Slaughter was having eggs and bacon when I arrived at the Dorchester the next morning. I no longer imagined it was funny to arrive in a raccoon coat and an odd hat. I read him some of my funniest sketches, while he drank coffee and munched his way through breakfast. George was a gigantic man with an enormous beard and a very loud laugh. He appeared to find everything about me amusing, fortunately this included my work.

'Listen,' confided George, as he tucked into his second kipper – he was a prodigious eater. 'Even if you don't write funny, you'll look funny, walking up and down the corridors, we've got a great writing office in the Toluca Capri Motel; you'll love the guys. You'll be partnered with Artie Johnson's identical twin brother Coslough, he's five feet tall. What are you? Six-three?'

'Four,' I said.

'Even better,' George said. 'We'll all get a laugh when you guys walk down the corridor.' It seemed a very strange premise for being a Hollywood writer, but that's Hollywood. Clearly if I had been shorter I wouldn't have stood a chance.

'You act as well?' said George.

'Yes.' I listed off the parts that I had already done. Then taking off my jacket, I squatted on my haunches and, pulling my sweater down to my ankles, walked round the table doing an impersonation of Toulouse-Lautrec. 'I'd love to be in the show,' I said, disappearing under the table and popping out the other side.

'A mad English man is just what we need,' said George, draining his coffe, 'Got a dinner jacket?'

'I have ze dinner jacket,' I said. 'I even have ze top hat.'

'It's the awards next week,' said George, 'you'd better come to those. Then we'll start you off with the boys for the new season.' Clapping me on the back, we parted. That was George. Unpredictable.

I returned to the Grafton Arms office.

'I got the job!' I said. 'I'm a writer on America's top show!'

'Hang on,' said the gallant Major. 'What's that? Two to one. I'll take it. Ten shillings each way, a cross double with the favourite in the four-thirty. Got what?' said the Major.

'I got the job,' I said. 'I'm off to Hollywood.'

'How much are they paying?' enquired the Major.

'Who cares,' I said. 'I'll do it for nothing.'

'You certainly won't do it for nothing,' said the gallant Major. 'I'm getting ten per cent of this.'

I packed my dinner jacket and took a suitcase full of comedy scripts and headed for fame in the very place I had sworn never to return to.

I was met at Los Angeles airport by a charming girl I had met during my assiduous pursuit of London nightlife, an actress called Julie Newmar, the original Catwoman in *Batman*. She was stunningly beautiful, over six feet tall and the pin-up of most American football teams. I had phoned her as soon as I got the job and she invited me to stay in her Hollywood apartment, as she was leaving to make a movie in New York. The apartment was just off Sunset Strip and the decor was Mexican, with lots of interesting plants, some of which I recognized as I had friends in London who were keen on smoking them, and a lovely sun terrace. I must admit I was rather demented about her and fortunately she was rather keen on me. I remember sitting up in bed, watching her do her exercises as she was a very athletic dancer, and thinking I hope I've got the strength for all this. Fortunately she had a great variety of vitamin pills; it was only later I discovered some of them were speed. I remember feeling very lively. She was also a very good sport and introduced me to her best friends before she departed. We kept in touch for quite a few years.

With that introduction, Hollywood seemed quite a lively place. But the Toluca Capri Motel was, however, quite a surprise. The five or six writers, who turned out America's top show, occupied almost the entire low building. The only original occupant being a very elderly lady, who refused to leave. Every morning the writers would type dramatic news items into the stop press column of her daily newspaper: ' . . . Alien beings land near Toluca Capri.' 'Killer chickens invade Hollywood. These chickens only eat elderly females and are heading for the Toluca Motel . . . '

The aged resident obviously never got as far as reading the stop press column, and seemed indifferent to the laughter and general mayhem, which would have driven any normal person totally bonkers.

There were either six or eight writers, I was never quite sure which. We worked in pairs. Each pair having their own office. The editor was a man called Paul Keyes, who kept himself apart from the rest of us. But the main driving force behind the whole operation was George Slaughter. It was quite a different situation to anything I had ever encountered before. We would have a meeting at dawn on Monday mornings, where brain-storming ideas were thrown about. At the meeting were the cast: Dick Martin and Dan Rowan, the hosts; Ruth Buzzi; Artie Johnson; Judy Carne – the original 'sock it to me girl' from London who, for those who like gossip, was going out with Burt Reynolds; Goldie Hawn and Alan Sues. George sat at the head of the table, conducting the show. We took it in turns to stand up and give our best ideas for comedic sketches. There was an endless list of people who wanted to be on the show, from Danny Kaye to Ronald Reagan, then Governor of California.

'Let's hear from the English boy,' said George, on my first morning.

I got up and suggested that we employ the Harlem Globe Trotters, dressed as Foreign Legionnaires, then book a number of midgets, and put them in Arab costume. The Legionnaires would then produce giant fly swats and swat the midgets.

'That's a terrible idea,' said George.

'Yes terrible,' echoed the other writers.

'Perhaps the worst idea we've ever heard, and for that idea you'll have to pay a penalty,' continued George.

'Cripes!' I said. 'What's that?'

'Well,' said George, 'every Monday morning, our good friend the motorcycle cop comes in here for a cup of tea and the latest gossip on the show. This morning, when he arrives, you will go out and disconnect his plug leads and he will be very displeased with you when he goes to start the bike.'

'How will he know it's me?'

''Cause,' said George, 'we will tell him. You'll be very unpopular.'

To my surprise our good friend the cop arrived, as he caught up on the gossip, I slipped out and removed his plug leads. The cop took his leave and returned abruptly, looking very unamused.

'Who's the wise guy?' he drawled. They all pointed at me.

He took out his notebook, and said he hoped I would enjoy a spell in the slammer. Needless to say, they had set this joke up beforehand. But it was a good introduction to their sense of humour. I found after a few weeks that writing a hundred gags before lunch was not an easy task, but thanks to being partnered with Coslough Johnson, Artie's twin brother, and my suitcase full of sketches, we usually managed to beat the deadlines. We got so good at writing quickly, that we had a recording made of busy typing, which we played while we had a long nap in the afternoons with the door locked.

I was constantly exhausted. Not only was I a writer on the show, I was also appearing in it. Some of the recording sessions would go on till three in the morning. Famous faces would pop in on their way home from an evening, just to do a line in a sketch. Faces that up to now I had only seen on the silver screen. I enjoyed every moment of it, until I had to do a sketch with Danny Kaye. It turned out to be something I had written with my partner and it wasn't going terribly well. Danny Kaye was standing with a lamp shade on his head, pretending to be a demented U-boat commander, while I was dressed as a housewife. Danny threw down the lampshade and asked who had written this crap? I had never met anybody who could use quite such descriptive language if things weren't going well. He got into a terrible rage and I hurriedly agreed that it was indeed crap and blamed two other writers. I joined him in the tantrum; he never knew I was partly responsible and I can tell you I never liked to get on the wrong side of Danny Kaye and prefer to remember him in *Wonder Man*.

I was even given time off to do a commercial, because by now the show was airing for twenty-six weeks of the year and I had become quite well known. I was asked to audition for a vegetable soup commercial. There was a large soup can on a raised platform and I was invited to climb a ladder, get inside, and lean out of the can, while a group of executives examined the result. I was cast as a string bean. There were other people who had been cast as different vegetables, but I was the first to audition.

'This the guy from *Laugh In*?' said somebody.

'Yep.'

'He doesn't look like a string bean to me.'

'Do I have any lines as the string bean?' I enquired, 'because if I have, I'm sure I could sound like a string bean.'

They ignored me. 'We could put a hat on him; he could do the mushroom.'

I was handed a large hat.

'He looks like a half-opened umbrella,' said a voice.

I almost got the part of the celery, who hadn't turned up, but in the end failed to be part of the famous vegetable soup commercial. I was very disappointed; it was my first real set back in Hollywood.

I did, however, go on game shows. All in all, I had a pretty remarkable time. The demands on the writers were quite intense, and one or two had nervous breakdowns and had to leave. They were quite unceremoniously dismissed as I recall. The door would open and somebody would say: 'Goodbye.' And the nervous person would disappear, to be replaced by another, equally nervous person. After the first year, I was quite an old hand. I thoroughly enjoyed my days away from the writing office, filming *Mad Moments* on a beach or golf course – in America's most popular TV series. By now I had moved from Miss Newmar's apartment into the house of Leslie Bricusse, writer of musicals, such as *Stop The World I Want To Get Off*, *Dr Doolittle* and many others. Leslie and his wife Evie looked after me in a mansion situated just behind the Beverly Hills Hotel, where I had been so unhappy, a few years before. I became rather good at pool, and was a nightly visitor to such hotspots as The Daisy and The Candy Store.

Girls were always very keen to come and see *Laugh In*, although it wasn't an audience show, and always asked me for invitations to attend. I remember George saying to me one day, 'How would you like to cast the dance sections in the show? You seem to know more pretty girls than our casting director.' I let it be known that I had been given the job of casting girls for the dance section in *Laugh In* and would be holding auditions on a Sunday morning. Leslie Bricausse still tells the story of how he came home at lunchtime to find sixty-five girls in the garden, each dancing to their own portable tape recorders, while I sat in dark glasses, under a large umbrella, making notes. I suppose I did get rather carried away.

Dancing late into the night one Friday probably saved my life. I had a call from Sharon Tate, the beautiful wife of Roman Polanski, the film director. I had met Roman and Sharon at the Saturday morning lunches at Alvaro's and become quite friendly with them. Sharon had arrived from London and was staying at a house nearby.

'Would you like to come over for tea on Saturday?'

'Yes, I would. Thanks Sharon. See you about four.'

I woke up well past midday on the Saturday and forgot all about her invitation. By that evening the occupants of that home had been brutally murdered by the Charles Manson Gang: it was a terrible shock to think that such a thing could happen. And I shudder even today when I think about it.

My second Christmas in Hollywood came round, and I was off to Acapulco. It was fairly unspoilt as it was in those days. I remember chatting on the beach with a tanned and lean Kirk Douglas. This beach was so private that they had a machine gunner at either end to make sure it wasn't invaded by revolutionaries. I also remember being invited to Merle Oberon's house. The remarkable thing about Merle Oberon is that she did look exactly like she did in her films: perfect and beautiful. She wore a white dress and her hair was tied up with a beautiful dark blue ribbon. I held her in my arms and we danced under the stars to a Mexican band with lots of fireworks going off. I was about to tell her how much I had enjoyed her movies when she told me excitedly how much she'd enjoyed seeing me in *Laugh In*. Being in a very popular show does have certain advantages. In my wildest dreams when dancing in a ballroom in Stoke Court to a wind-up gramophone, and sitting in the cinema as a paint salesman, I never imagined that one day I would be leading this sort of life. It wasn't as if I had planned it. It just happened. Water skiing, parties every night, smoking interesting plants, making new friends, I thought it would never end. I got so brown I was invisible at night, except for my teeth. Six weeks later, I returned to Hollywood to start the next season.

England seemed a long way away. You're probably wondering what happened to Grandma. Well, I didn't leave her. She left me. She died peacefully before I left England in Mount Vernon Hospital, in what seemed a very tiny cot and I held her hand and kept talking to her, long after she had passed away. As I was leaving at about three o'clock in the morning, a voice called out: 'Is that you Bobby?' I turned to see another elderly lady, who appeared to be expecting a visit from her son. I sat on her bed and held her hand. I'm quite sure she had no idea that I wasn't her son. She talked about the good times we had had, before she went to sleep. I hope somebody will come and see me if ever I am lying in one of those little cots. It must be very lonely waiting for the end without someone to reminisce with.

Once back in Beverly Hills, I returned to what writers call the grindstone, but what for me was just great fun. I had letters from friends in England, who had seen me on television and even one from my father, saying that even he had seen me. He wrote how pleased he was that I was getting on well and hoped I was saving money. It was rather cheering. Leslie's house was always full of famous people. Quite often I played the mad English butler in false whiskers at his dinner parties: spilling soup on people and generally acting the fool. It sounds a bit ridiculous now, but it was great fun at the time. I had become quite an extrovert.

Fred Astaire lived next door, but to my disappointment I never actually saw him. My mother told me that she once danced in a show with him in London, called *Blue Skies*. Years later, Leslie gave him one of my poetry books and Fred wrote a charming letter in which he remembered meeting my mother whom he fondly referred to as a Margo Lees, which was her maiden name.

Half way through that second year I returned to England for a brief visit, during which time I met the lovely Joanna Lumley. This wasn't actually the first time I had met her. A few years before I had attended a party one evening and noticed her. However, I wasn't introduced at the time. This time our meeting was slightly strange as we were both cast in a movie, in which I was playing a lady. I was in a costumier's, wearing net stockings and a red dress, when she knocked on the door and said, 'Hello, Jeremy. I believe we're doing a movie together.'

'Excuse me,' I said. 'I'm in the middle of changing.'

The first time we were introduced I was at a slight disadvantage, although she did compliment me on my legs. Her acting career hadn't really taken off at that time and she was still modelling for Jean Muir. Though I think she had had a part in a film called *The Breaking Of Bumbo*, which never got a showing as far as I remember. Anyway we were both unattached, and had a whirlwind romance. I must say based mainly on a sense of humour. She is quite the most amusing girl anyone could meet.

We got married at Chelsea Registry Office and I moved in to her flat in Holland Park. We planned to return to America, where I would continue writing and appearing in the show. At the last moment, Joanna decided that America wasn't a good place to bring up her son, Jamie. We argued about it for a while, but she was adamant. I then made a bad career move and sent a cable resigning from *Laugh In*. Cables were sent back: 'Come home, we love you!' But the die had been cast.

We settled instead for an extended honeymoon at a lovely villa in the South of France, at St Paul de Vence. The villa had once been a restaurant and had an enormous old barbecue in the gardens. We gave some great parties. Jack Davis, who had started my film career was by then living nearby and together we worked on an idea for a TV series, which we managed to sell some years later.

At the end of a wonderful summer Joanna and I realized we had both married in a hurry. That is to say she realized she had married in a hurry. I think I married because I thought it was the last chance I was going to get, because by now I was forty and becoming a hypochondriac. I suspected that the headless horseman would appear over the hills at any moment. I was also broke. In fact, I was so desperate for work I agreed to rewrite Jimmy Clithero's stage act.

Jimmy Clithero was a diminutive performer who played an eternal child. Though by the time I got to his act, which arrived on yellowed pages, he was quite aged. I was to be paid a hundred pounds. I worked feverishly and wrote him into the twentieth century with a spanking new act. I phoned him up in Blackpool where he lived to see if he had read this effort. His mother answered the phone.

'I'm afraid Jimmy's having his dinner.'

'Has he read the new act?'

'Yes, he has; he'll tell you about it after dinner.'

'What's he having for dinner?'

'Fish.'

'Is it a big fish?' I was really desperate to speak to Jimmy. He promised to call me back; he never did. He died. Not from the fish, I hasten to add, but certainly a short while later.

The only thing I really regret is that Joanna, in a moment of pique, quite understandable I'm sure, because I can be very aggravating, threw away my treasured photograph albums of all my pictures of Hollywood, and highlights of my career. I think that the main reason she did this was that a lot included quite pretty girls with whom I worked. I would probably have done the same in her place. But Joanna Lumley of the wonderful teeth is still one of the most kind, engaging and amusing people I have ever met, and we still do meet occasionally. And I'm thrilled she has had had such a successful career. From time to time her voice still haunts me on television commercials, as I lie dozing in front of the fire, before I go out dancing.

At this stage one crisis after another seemed to overtake me. As my marriage ended, so did my father's life, in a most unfortunate way. He had fallen out of bed during the night and slept on the floor next to an electric fire, which automatically switched itself on at 6.00 a.m. He was still fast asleep when his wife found him an hour later. Joanna came with me to the hospital. The doctors had given him twenty-four hours at the most. He was very brave and told me I had done terribly well and he was really proud of me. He asked me to make sure he had plenty of cigarettes as he was determined to smoke till the end. We said goodbye. I cried all the way home, and I never saw him again. There was another cable waiting for me saying, 'Come back to Hollywood, we love you.' I had a nervous breakdown instead.

Nervous breakdowns are strange things. You're quite aware you are having one, but there is nothing you can do about it. A friend had just bought a house and allowed me to stay in it. It was virtually without furniture, apart from a couple of beds and a bean bag. I stayed in the spare room, somewhere off Kensington High Street and used to write notes to myself and place them on the mirror, such as: 'Cheer up, it's going to be all right'. But I remember I cried a lot for a long time. I didn't feel like I could work, I didn't feel I could do anything. I was also broke. I had nightmares that I was back on the road selling paint.

It was clear my life was over. I contemplated suicide, but spent so long writing a heart-rending note that I got a headache and went to bed with two junior aspirins. I think that when things are really bad, you are supposed to phone your friends and they're supposed to comfort you. But I didn't like to tell anybody that this egocentric mad idiot had got his come-uppance and stayed on my own. I did manage to write a short story about seven pregnant men for which I got about £1200 from an American producer. I phoned Jack Davis in the South of France. Did he still want to sell his lovely dark blue Silver Cloud Rolls-Royce? Yes, he did. I took the train down to the

South of France and bought it for a thousand, enjoyed the sunshine for a week, and then drove back to London, hoping to sell the Rolls and make a bit of profit, but I liked it so much I decided to hang onto it and with that extravagant gesture, my luck seemed to change.

I wrote a short outline about life in a department store, based loosely on my own, and sent it to the heads of major television companies. I also sent one copy to David Croft, the writer of *Dad's Army*, whom I had met briefly when Joanna and I did a six-part television show together called *It's Awfully Bad For Your Eyes, Darling!* It was about three girls living in a flat. I also lived in the flat as Joanna's boyfriend, who had to be hidden from her mother. Not a bad bit of typecasting really, but it was a rather strange situation because we had just got divorced. I was also allowed to do a bit of script-editing on the show and managed to write in things for Joanna to do, which really annoyed her, such as ironing my shirt, cooking my breakfast and always agreeing with me. The show never really took off, but I wish I could get hold of a copy as it was really great fun to do.

Anyway, David Croft liked the idea of the department store and invited me to lunch at his large house in Holland Park. We discussed the sort of characters we would need, and David agreed we should write the show. He was also going to produce and direct it. And so *Are You Being Served?* was born.

Are You Being Served? was the first big success I had with the BBC. And working with David Croft was just one big laugh. We would take it in turns to write. He'd have a pad on his knee and I'd talk and do the jokes. Then I would take the pad and he'd do the same. In latter years he spent more time with the pad than I did, because my writing was slower than his.

'Let's get it down,' he used to say. 'Let's get it down.'

Then, as we passed page twenty-eight, I'd say, 'We're writing for the waste-paper basket.' And we would stop.

It has never been hard work with David. People often ask if the actors add lines and I think they will agree, it happens very seldom. But what they give is their great professionalism. And I couldn't ask to have worked with more professional people than Molly Sugden, Frank Thornton, John Inman or Arthur Brough, who interestingly enough just seem to be variations of their normal selves in the show. Wendy Richards, on the other hand, really is just like herself in the show and has a very dry sense of humour behind that cigarette holder and those electric blue eyes. Trevor Bannister and Nicholas Smith, of course, completed the cast. It was very sad during the series to lose Arthur Brough, who played Mr Grainger; a very hard man to replace in life, never mind in a show. Arthur English too, was a wonderful character and still is. I keep hoping he will pop up in the new series of *Grace and Favour* at some point.

Young Mr Grace, played by Harold Bennett was a wonderful invention. I always remember when he was being auditioned for the part – he was then probably in his late eighties – he said, 'Do you want me to use my old man's voice?' which was a slightly more quavery version of his own. Never in the best of health, he was such an endearing old gentleman, one forgave him completely for chasing pretty nurses. We used to do quite outrageous jokes when I look back, like dear young Mr Grace, acquiring a pace-maker with a little pole with a red light on top, which would indicate whether he was under undue strain. He would then call a nurse in, in a short skirt, and ask her to bend down and put the electric kettle on. He would bang his equipment vigorously, and when it didn't light up she was fired. Real McGill Postcard stuff. But much loved by the audience. Not to mention the writers. They also loved it in a lot of other countries, and I believe it once held up the opening of the Israeli Parliament for a while, as the members were so keen on the show which was running over a bit. True or not, it made a good story in the newspapers.

There was a slight hiccup in the production when David had a heart attack. I went to see him in hospital, where he was connected up to machine. However, when two comedy writers meet it's very hard not to crack a joke. And I was asked to leave shortly afterwards, as he was laughing so much; his life-support system was in danger of blowing up. But fortunately he made a good recovery by which time the show had attracted the eye of the American producers. So David and I flew to Hollywood to set up production of *Beans of Boston*, the Americanized version, under the guidance of Mr Herman Rush, one of the legends of American television and until recently the President of Columbia Television. Gary Marshall, the man behind *Happy Days*, was the executive producer. David and I had our names in the studio car park, and also on our office door, except mine was spelt 'Geremy'. But I didn't mind, I was about to become a big wheel. I also had a very nice girlfriend at the time called Jo Wynn, who was living in Los Angeles.

David and I were given poolside rooms at the Beverly Wilshire Hotel. It really was true Hollywood – luxury. Each morning we would drive through the rather acid-filled air and bright sunshine past the palm trees to the studio and our production office, where we held auditions and met the two American writers, who had been assigned to the show. As usual David wrote the signature tune and I was allowed to do the lyrics. This took quite a long time to record. And we also had to discuss the art work for the opening titles of the show. We were really involved from every aspect.

We saw a lot of actors, including Robin Williams, though it was before he found the fame he has today. We thought he was terribly good, but couldn't think what to do with him. We also met one of the surviving Ritz Brothers. Similar to the Marx Brothers, the Ritz Brothers had been around almost from the time of silent movies. I thought it rather remarkable to find oneself actually speaking to one of them.

A wizened little old man in a very smart suit, Harry Ritz came for the part of young Mr Grace. He was about the same age as Harold Bennett, but not in such good shape. The man on the gate of the studio was too young to remember the Ritz Brothers, and he made Harry Ritz leave his car outside the lot and walk across the studio complex to the office. As the studio complex was vast and the office was at the top of a long flight of stairs, it was about fifteen minutes before Harry Ritz could speak. We were very concerned about his health and I remember we drove him back to his car in an electric golf cart that we borrowed. Gary Marshall decreed that our sort of Mr Grace was too old and that they would look for a younger man, who would play an older man, which is typical American double-thinking. Alan Sues was recruited from the now defunct cast of *Laugh In* to play John Inman's part as Mr Humphreys. I had forgotten quite how mad he was and this probably turned out to be a bit of miscasting. An actor called John Hellerman had been elected to play Frank Thornton's part and at the read through for these chosen people, we all sat waiting for his arrival. He didn't arrive. Gary Marshall suggested that I should read the part of Captain Peacock. I did this in my best English acting voice and knowing the character very well, got quite a few laughs.

'You've got the part,' said Gary Marshall.

'What?' said David Croft, aghast. 'He can't do it! He's busy writing.'

'Please,' I said. 'This is my great chance.'

David was adamant. J. Lloyd would not be playing Captain Peacock. Fortunately John Hellerman did turn up eventually. He was very good. Nevertheless, Gary Marshall had been impressed and offered me a part in *Happy Days* as an English lawyer. Unfortunately, they wrote *Happy Days* so far ahead the part wasn't available for another three months. I said I would do it at the time, but I wasn't to know that in three months time I would be back in England. Nevertheless, it was very exciting making an American show.

David and I became very friendly with Herman Rush and his wife and one evening we were invited to dinner. I took my friend Miss Wynn along. We had a very enjoyable evening, though I don't remember what we actually had to eat. But due to the food provided by the kind Mrs Rush, or something else, I don't know exactly, but by two o'clock in the morning, I had such a pain that I had to call the hotel doctor, who gave me a shot of something. By six o'clock in the morning I was still in agony. An ambulance was called and I sped off in it to the Cedars Hospital, accompanied by Jo Wynn, whom David Croft had called to say that her friend was probably on the way out.

The hospital was like a hotel. I remember arriving at the reception on a stretcher and being asked for my credit card. I didn't have one. They needed a thousand dollars immediately before I could be admitted. Dear Jo came to my rescue with the aid of American Express. I was taken up in the lift and wheeled along on a trolley. A beaming black nurse told me that Walter Pidgeon was dying in the room next to mine. I was sad to hear the news, but also glad that it wasn't Walter being wheeled along, and hearing a similar fate had befallen me.

I was there for about five days, while every test imaginable was carried out. It wasn't till some years later that I discovered I had had a burst ulcer. But by the time they finished these tests I was positively glowing with barium. During my stay I had a visit from two executives at the studio. I hadn't met them before, but they entered my room enthusiastically with a basket of fruit.

'We're from the studio,' said the first one. 'We're really deeply worried about you, Geoffrey, and we've brought you this fruit.'

I didn't like to mention that my name wasn't Geoffrey. I wondered if they'd got the wrong room.

'*Beans* is going great,' said the second one.

They had got the right room. They were still wishing me well as they left. I thought it was time I enquired what the cost was to date; I phoned up the accounts department. It was run by a certain Mr Lash, who had a sort of robotic voice. He sounded as though he was speaking from a flying saucer somewhere high above the earth.

'When the clock strikes twelve, it will be four thousand dollars.'

'Good heavens,' I said. 'I can't possibly afford that.' By now I did have access to some funds, but if twelve was going to be the bewitching hour that removed an extra thousand dollars from my account, I was going to leave, and I told him so.

'You can't leave,' said the voice. 'You'll never make it in time.'

It was indeed difficult. I was connected up to some tubing, which disappeared into my arm from a bottle on a stand. I phoned the faithful Miss Wynn and told her I intended to escape. Could she bring a car around to the back entrance? She promised to be there in five minutes, and it was about quarter to twelve. I left the room propelling the stand along in front of me, still connected to the liquid in the bottle – I'm not sure what it was, but I'm sure it was very expensive. The nurse asked where I was going. I told her – out.

'You have to leave on a trolley,' she said. I found a trolley, climbed on it with the stand, pushed against the wall and propelled myself into a goods lift, pressed the button and descended. I arrived in a sort of cargo bay. Propelling myself out of the lift, I found I'd hit an incline and sped down at some speed, much to the surprise of the driver of the medical delivery vehicle, who was just pulling up. Jo Wynn duly arrived and I detached myself from the equipment and sped back to the hotel. I got so elated about escaping that I phoned Mr Lash to tell him I had made an escape before twelve o'clock. It hadn't been recorded, he said, so I couldn't have gone out past reception. I explained, I had left by the delivery entrance. He told me it didn't count but he'd give me an A + for trying. The bill was duly sent and I paid it. Unfortunately, *Beans of Boston* was not a great success as a pilot and was not picked up. But fortunately, I had made a great friend in Mr Herman Rush. So this was not the end of our relationship.

Some months later I got a call from him. Could I come back? He was now the President of Columbia Television and had taken option on my book, *The Adventures of Captain Dangerfield* – a sort of 'Secret Life of Walter Mitty' published by W. H. Allen, which I had written on my return from *Laugh In*. And once again I found myself at the Beverly Wilshire Hotel on a Sunday evening, sitting at the bar, looking forward to meeting him at seven o'clock the next morning for one of those breakfast meetings where one is at one's most inspired. They were thinking of putting a version of my book into a well-known show at the time called *Fantasy Island*, starring Ricardo Montalban. And although it was only going to be one episode of *Fantasy Island*, it would be a step into a Hollywood television series and so I was very excited at the prospect.

As I sat at the bar, I became aware of a woman staring at me. She had a briefcase on her knee, and was drinking coffee at a table nearby. I smiled. She smiled back, and indicated I should join her.

'You're alone?' she said.

'Yes,' I said. 'I'm a writer here to meet a person at Columbia Television.'

'I'm waiting for someone,' she said, 'who hasn't arrived.'

'Ah,' I said, 'that can happen.'

'Are you interested in extraterrestrials?'

'Yes,' I said. At seven o'clock in the evening there wasn't much happening. I thought one might as well be interested in extraterrestrials as anything else. Apart from which I had read avidly anything to do with flying saucers, having once spotted one, when cycling in Northwood. I didn't realize it at the time; I just thought the government had invented a large saucer-shaped object which had flown overhead. It was many years later when I started reading about flying saucers, that I realized I had been very privileged to observe one. It had been, no doubt, having a closer look at life in Middlesex.

'I belong to a communications group,' she said. The way she addressed me one would have thought we knew each other terribly well. I did think for a moment I was being picked up, but she opened her briefcase and produced pictures of beings from another planet. That is to say, she *said* they were beings from another planet. They were certainly tall and appeared to be standing in the desert. There were two or three of them. They could easily have been people covered in white sheets; but they were rather fuzzy and indistinct. So it was hard to say whether they were real or not.

'We photographed these people after we made contact. This is the Mojave Desert,' she said.

I nodded. I looked around. There were a few people drinking and chatting. And here I was looking at alien beings. And I'd only been in the hotel a short time. Still, pretty typical, I suppose.

'How did you meet them?' I said.

'We contact them mentally,' she said.

'And where are they from?'

'Venus.'

'Ah.'

She looked at her watch. 'I was expecting a Russian professor; he's very interested in our work. I don't know what could have held him up. It could have been the others.'

'The others?'

'Yes, there are travellers from other worlds who don't like us being friendly with these people from Venus. They're constantly trying to interrupt our communications.'

'There's always a fly in the ointment,' I said.

'We have a communication plan for tonight; it's on the top of Look-out Mountain. There are three of us. We really need four. Would you be free?'

'You mean would you like me to come to Look-out Mountain to meet some people from Venus?'

'They may not come,' she said. 'As far as we can tell, they should be here by midnight.'

I would like to point out that by now at least an hour and a half had elapsed when I had talked using my extensive knowledge about these types of phenomena.

'I'm not doing anything this evening. Yes I could, I could come along, I suppose.'

In about forty minutes she had driven me to a small house

in the Hollywood Hills. And I found myself in the company of a Japanese gentleman with rather thick glasses, and an ex-Vietnam flyer. The room was completely covered with photographs of extraterrestrial beings, flying saucers and unexplained objects. They didn't seem too pleased that she had brought me along. They cross-examined me closely about such things as the Philadelphia Experiment. Did I know about it? Yes, I was ready to discuss all the details of the Philadelphia Experiment. I could go on Mastermind about such useless information. They seemed quite impressed.

I now regretted starting this venture, but they were so enthusiastic, I didn't like to ask if I could call a cab. So I joined them in the back of a pick-up truck and we headed for the top of Look-out Mountain. It was quite a tall peak and it took quite a long time to get there. In fact, it wasn't far off midnight when we arrived. I shuddered to think of what state I would be in in the morning for the breakfast meeting with Mr Herman Rush, who incidentally doesn't know this story. They talked so enthusiastically and knowledgeably about these meetings that I almost began to believe that they had had them.

We parked the truck and they picked up binoculars. Opening up a box they brought out four little helmets, painted gold and with a point on top.

'We need these to concentrate,' I was told. 'Put yours on and think hard. And look at this picture of the flying saucer and think hard.'

My main thought was that I only had about eleven cigarettes on me and if anybody did arrive from Venus it was probably a non-smoking planet, which would be a disadvantage. Nevertheless, I did say I would concentrate.

Although I concentrated very hard, very little seemed to happen, until nearly one o'clock. Then a bright light shot up in the sky. It was probably a shooting star, but I was so hyped up by then, I was quite sure something of an extraterrestrial nature was happening. I suddenly became genuinely concerned that I might well be abducted. Never having had a reputation for being unreliable, I made my new-found companions promise that should I be taken off by aliens either for experiment or pleasure, they would phone the Beverly Wilshire Hotel to alert Mr Herman Rush to the fact that I would not be appearing in the Pink Turtle Lounge at seven o'clock as arranged the following morning, due to unforeseen circumstances. They promised to do this.

Ten minutes later, there was a red, white and blue light flashing in the distance, heading inexorably in our direction, climbing very gradually as it came into view. By now I was convinced that, under the guidance of an extraterrestrial force, it had been arranged for me to be in this place at this time. The purpose of my whole life became clear. I was to be taken to another planet as an example of a perfectly normal earthling. I nervously took off my helmet in an effort to retain some anonymity when the beings arrived. Along quite a clear stretch of road, a light appeared about eight feet above the ground and headed in our direction. I wished that I had never entered upon this adventure. The light passed by on top of an ambulance. I breathed a sigh of relief. As far as I was concerned this had been a very close encounter of the worst kind and once again I had let my vivid imagination run away with me. Useful to have as a writer, but dangerous in the real world.

I think I got back to the hotel about five o'clock in the morning, and was rather listless at the meeting and didn't like to mention to Mr Rush that I had been up most of the night. This, however, did not make any difference to whether *Captain Dangerfield* was used in an episode of *Fantasy Islnd. Fantasy Island* was cancelled, but my friendship with Herman Rush remained.

9

Are You Being Served? continued to run for ten years; and during this time, in the mid-seventies, I moved into a small cottage in St James's, next door to St James's Palace. Built in 1642, it had an original gas lamp outside and lots of wooden beams. I used some of my grandmother's furniture and created a comfortable bolt hole.

While I was writing *Are You Being Served?* an old friend of mine, Lance Percival, came up with a very good idea for a detective series called *Whodunnit?*, which I co-wrote with him. We made them for Thames Television. Jon Pertwee was the anchor man; the same Jon Pertwee that I had met years ago in my early days. He was already popular as Doctor Who and an ideal person for the part. We had a panel of experts trying to solve the crimes we wrote; the experts, of course, being well-known actors or actresses, which included Patrick Mower, and Anouska Hempel as resident panellists. Anouska was particularly good at solving crimes, but then she is good at everything, particularly decor. She created Blake's Hotel in Roland Gardens, the 'in' place for show business people. Apart from that, she has her own fashion house and perfume company; quite a remarkable lady.

The idea of the programme was that the murder scene should

be played out and then the actors would all be cross-examined by the panel, who would hopefully solve the crime. *Whodunnit?* proved quite a success, and ran for five years. Then Lance and I went to Hollywood and made about eighteen *Whodunnit?*s for American television. This time it was a game show with a $64,000 prize. F. Lee Bailey and Marvin Belli, two famous American lawyers, each represented a team of amateur detectives picked from an audience; it was a hair-raising experience. Lance and I used to be locked in a dressing room while the contestants were picked, so we couldn't tip off anybody in the show – not that we would have. We were too busy worrying if we had made the clues too hard. We had already had a nasty moment with Marvin, who'd been very aggravated about the clues, asking how was he supposed to solve them when they were so obscure. Nevertheless, we also managed to pursue a fairly relentless social life, which had a slight hiccup when Lance had a date with a girl whose sex was questionable.

'I'd like you to meet her,' said Lance. 'I've got a feeling she might be a man, after all you can never be sure.'

'I'll come with you,' I said, 'and if I suspect the *slightest hint* of masculinity, I'll somehow introduce the name of a football club into the conversation – subtly of course.'

'Of course,' said Lance.

Lance rang the bell of the apartment and a gorgeous blonde opened the door and said, 'Hello, boys.'

'Manchester United,' I said.

Lance collapsed. I had recognized a drag artist who turned out to be a very amusing dinner date. Tinsel town was always full of surprises. But then so is London.

Back home in London, my new cottage at Russell Court was rather spooky at night. I remember one New Year's Eve, I was sitting writing a show – I'm not very fond of New Year's Eve so I had decided to work through the night. Just after midnight I heard the squeak of a window being raised. I realized immediately that I was about to be burgled. I crawled to the curtains on all fours to observe the would-be burglar's nose, pressing against the closed curtains, and a hand appearing over the windowsill. I cursed not having a dog. Whipping the curtains aside, I gave a loud bark. Unfortunately for the burglar my teeth clamped on his nose, giving him one hell of a shock. It was the second time I had bitten somebody on the nose. I seemed to be getting better at it. The burglar turned out to be over seventy years old and he collapsed onto the cobblestones. I brought him in and had to revive him with a brandy. He confessed it was the worst setback he had had in his burgling career, which from his description had been extensive. I helped him to the corner of St James's Street, where we found a cab, which incidentally I paid for. He lived not unsurprisingly somewhere in Islington. He thanked me profusely as he climbed aboard, promising never to do me again.

I found myself lunching with a film producer, called Jack Weiner, to show him my new script about Count Dracula, which he read that afternoon. Later, he gave me a call and said he thought David Niven would be ideal for it. In fact, he'd already called Niven in the South of France. It appeared that David Niven had always wanted to play Count Dracula. So the trip to meet one of my heroes was arranged. Jack and I flew into Nice, hired a car and drove to David's house, a beautiful villa set in a thirteenth-century olive grove on a small peninsula on the Mediterranean.

It was a wonderfully hot day and my first meeting with David was in the garden; he came out in shirtsleeves, holding a bottle of champagne in one hand and three glasses in the other, as debonair in life as he was in the movies.

'Let's get this straight old chap, it's Jeremy and David, isn't it?' He handed me a glass and poured.

Niven was somebody who could make anybody feel at home immediately. We sat in the garden and discussed the film idea. He reiterated the fact that he had always wanted to play Count Dracula. I told him how *Dawn Patrol* – the World War One flying epic that he'd also been in with Errol Flynn – had made such an impression on me.

'Really, old chap. I've got lots of photographs of that.' We retired indoors and he brought out beautifully bound photograph albums with a complete record of his career. I wished I could be tidy like that. I start an album, then all the pages drop out, and I end up with a few photographs in a drawer. This was before he wrote *The Moon's a Balloon*, and the way he described his adventures with Flynn and Hollywood in the old days made us roar with laughter. There was no doubt all he had to do was actually sit down and write to have a bestseller, which of course he did.

David arrived in London and the film was made. There were lots of pretty girls in it and they all fell in love with him. The first ten minutes of the film were very funny. After that whenever I wanted to put comedy in, such as Count Dracula inventing the collapsible top hat so he could get into his coffin, Mr Weiner the producer wanted scenes of *Grand Guignol* proportions with lots of blood. I think really my best line in the whole film was where David, as a modern-day Dracula, is sitting looking at *Playboy*. He pulls out the centrefold and stares at it and remarks to his butler: 'My word, what a splendid pair of jugulars!'

I hasten to add this wasn't the tone of the whole film. Some of it was actually *very* funny. Nevertheless, the great thing was that it was actually made and I remember turning up on the opening night wearing a Dracula cloak, which Niven had given me. I was one of the few people in the audience, because the company had decided to open it on the night of the General Election of that year. So, as they say, it sank without trace, only to reappear some years later, on American television, retitled *Old Dracula*, and become quite a cult hit. Needless to say, no cheques were received from this exposure. The best thing about the film was the fact that Niven and I became very friendly and I still have a charming letter from him, saying how much he and his wife enjoyed *Are You Being Served?*. Apparently they were in London and on their way to an important dinner party and were late because of it. In fact, we corresponded or saw each other up until the time of his sad death from motor neurone disease, which had left him unable to sign even a letter.

A far more successful film about vampires was *Love at First Bite*, starring George Hamilton, which I wish I had written. I only mention this, because I did actually write a bit of it. I was sitting in a restaurant in Los Angeles when George Hamilton arrived in the middle of shooting with an attractive girl. George was usually seen with an attractive girl. We greeted each other with the usual show business enthusiasm.

'How's the film going?' I said.

'Big problem with the love scene,' said George. 'Got to work on it.'

I had just finished my lunch and offered to have a look at the script. I did so, while George tucked into his lunch, changing his verbal gears from charming to extremely charming. In two hours I had made copious notes on the back of three menus and inserted them into the script. George read my notes. 'Wonderful,' he said. 'You've solved our problem. We're going to use all this.' He departed without even offering to pay for my lunch.

Out of the blue, I got a call from a publisher, who had apparently heard Keith Michell on radio recounting his life, in the course of which he'd mentioned his stint at the Lyric as Robert Browning in *Robert and Elizabeth* and the existence of a writer/actor called Jeremy Lloyd, who had written some amusing poems about animals and insects, which he'd illustrated. He'd even read one or two on the radio programme. I had forgotten all about them. I had indeed used to write poems. In fact, I was rather good at making up things like that. The publisher wanted to know if I had any more. I said I had.

The publisher was really a record producer with a lot of contacts in the record and book world, by the name of Jonathan

Rowlands. I met him for a coffee and he gave me a record, which he'd produced. It was called 'Banana Blush' and contained John Betjeman's poems set to music, and read by Betjeman himself. The music was composed by Jim Parker. I found it very charming and I thought the music was terrific. I searched through my files and found a lot of poems I had written, mostly for my own amusement and that of my friends, and gave them to him.

Jim Parker duly composed the music, and then we had to find artists who would sing or speak them. By then I'd got quite a list of friends who were in show business and I approached Peter Sellers, Twiggy, Harry Secombe, Petula Clarke, Gordon Jackson and others who readily agreed that they would perform. No one worried very much about fees; they just enjoyed doing it. We had great fun at the recording studio, particularly with Peter Sellers who had, amongst his many talents, the remarkable ability to sing off key in a Jamaican accent. Then I needed a title song. I remembered once being called 'Beaky' at school and I decided that a bird called Captain Beaky should feature in the title song, together with animals such as Reckless Rat, Timid Toad and Artful Owl, ball pitted against an adversary called Hissing Sid the Snake.

I think I wrote the title song in one inspired session. It was rushed to the studio where it was recorded by Keith Michell, who at that time was the director of the Chichester Theatre. He also agreed to do the illustrations for a book. My original contract had included a book deal, so I was very pleased that my work would be read as well as listened to. The result, as Doctor Dunwell might have expected, was an immediate failure. Nobody seemed to have heard of the record and the book didn't attract much attention either. 'Captain Beaky' vanished without trace.

It was at this time that *Are You Being Served?* was very popular in Australia and they wanted to make their own version. I was elected to go over, and produce and write six shows, starring John Inman, surrounded by Australian actors. I duly left for Australia. I can't say I enjoyed it enormously, but I did enjoy the Sydney Barbies. I had a fish lunch at Double Bay, which is expected, and a terrible bout of toothache. After some primitive root canal work, I collapsed outside the dentist's on a large patch of grass in a park. I was lying there with a frozen jaw in the hot Australian morning sun, when a voice said, 'Hello handsome. I just love that velvet jacket. By the way, my name's Barbara.'

I opened my eyes to find a group of interested young men, staring at me. I tried to explain I was an English visitor making a television show, but unfortunately my jaw was still paralysed. I got up and ran. A voice shouted: ' "The Lord said let there be love in the world" Cobber. Surely we can be friends.'

I hailed a taxi and wrote down the name of my hotel, unable to communicate in any other way, despite convulsive movements of my jaw.

'Blimey,' said the driver. 'Another one! And all in velvet. Get in.'

I returned from Australia to find that 'Captain Beaky' was a great hit, thanks to Noel Edmonds, who'd been playing it every Sunday on his radio show. I was very grateful for this unexpected help as Noel and I had fallen out slightly a year or two before, when as a writer and actor I had been invited to participate in a race to be held the same day as the British Grand Prix at Brands Hatch. This was a show business race promoted by the Lords Taverners Society and some well-known faces attended, including Noel Edmonds, who had quite a reputation as a fast driver on race tracks, and also as I recall Johnny Dankworth, Nicholas Parsons, and the handsome actor who played the lead in *Hadley*, Gerald Harper, as well as one or two other great car nuts.

The cars were all standard Ford Mexicos and used as demonstrators by the circuit racing school. There were about twenty entrants.

Since my Lotus 6 days, I hadn't been on a track. Determined to do well, I drove down to Brands Hatch in a new acquisition, a Sid Lawrence Bentley Special; this was a chopped down affair with a four and a quarter litre engine and a two-seater body, which did about nought to fifty in four seconds. I always drove this with the windscreen down, wearing goggles. Errol Flynn in *Dawn Patrol* still had left a deep impression on my mind. I practised daily on the Grand Prix circuit. I don't suppose the Ford Mexicos did much more than ninety flat out. But I can tell you, an opposite lock round, and the corners, accompanied by the howl of the tyres as they tried to release themselves from the track really got that old adrenalin going, and I was putting in some pretty good practice times. On the day of the race, I drove down with some friends; they had special t-shirts made with the name 'Captain Dangerfield' emblazoned upon them, because I always saw myself as that sort of character. It was quite clear I was having great difficulty in growing into adult life and had progressed from a twit into a big-headed twit. We were briefed by famous racing drivers.

'Any advice?' I said.

'Give 'em arseholes,' I was told. I took this enigmatic advice to heart.

We lined up on the grid. It was only then that I realized I had brought my reading glasses. These were fine to read the instruments; and pretty good up to twelve feet beyond the end of the bonnet. After that things started to get a bit hazy. I desperately searched inside my overalls. No, I'd definitely brought the wrong glasses. I didn't actually see the green light go on, but as everyone started off, I started off too. I remember arriving at the first corner; it seemed to appear before I actually saw it, which was in much faster time that I'd ever been round it in practice. I came out sideways and kept my foot on the floor, as I went through the gears, only to find that the next right-hander had arrived equally quickly. Fortunately, there were one or two people in front of me, and I realized that, if I kept within ten or twelve feet of the tail of the car in front, I would be able to follow them around the track. It happened to be the tail of Noel Edmonds' car. As he was faster than anybody else, so was I. The crowd had turned out to see the British Grand Prix, and the whole of the track was lined with seemingly cheering, waving people. I lost count of the number of laps and although they were held up on large boards by the start, I was unable to make out which lap I was on. I hung grimly onto the tail of Noel's car, although I didn't know it was him in it at the time. To my surprise I found I was making up a bit of distance and managed to get alongside. I peered over the top of my glasses to see who it was. It was only then that I recognized him. Just as I looked, he drove into me. I thought he had probably had a stroke or something. But apparently it was quite normal to drive into people to put them off their stride. I found him on my outside on a long left-hander, heading up for the bridge. I placed my car on his inside and drove into him. He disappeared from view and I was alone. I didn't realize it, but I was now leading the race. Unfortunately, I couldn't really see where I was going, until the corners arrived. This meant that I went round them extremely quickly. I was going sideways a lot of the time. I was just heading for a very tight bend which I saw at the last moment, when there was a thump in the rear and Noel Edmonds sped past me, as I spun, turned over and hung in my safety harness – just as I had done years before, when my pram turned over. He won the race and I got the fastest lap. I wanted to kill him at the time, but soon got over it. I've still got the document which says 'Fastest Lap'; it's on faded yellow paper.

After that they gave up allowing amateurs like myself to race on the Grand Prix circuit. They confine the races now just to the club circuit, so with luck my fastest lap will remain intact. Apparently, I impressed one of the manufacturers who offered me a drive in a works-sponsored car. I declined. I thought I had been lucky to survive. Unlike the days of the gallant Major who photographed me through a camera obscura, the event was indelibly recorded for television and I still have the tape. I am always pleased when the commentator says: 'And now Lloyd is door-handling Edmonds. This boy's obviously done it before. Yes, he's past him and he's up and away.'

Noel, on the other hand, when I spoke to him about it at the time he was playing 'Captain Beaky', said he remembered the event well; he thought apparently, at the time, I was perhaps the most dangerous driver he had ever come across. He'd only let me past him, because he had a career ahead of him. I explained about my glasses, and we had a laugh about it. Anyway, Noel promoted 'Captain Beaky' relentlessly.

I was of course surprised to have such sudden notoriety as a writer of children's books and songs. Even more so as a second book was ordered immediately and another record planned. This meant that the little cottage at Russell Court had frequent visitors. For instance, Jim Parker, the composer, would often come over. I had a piano there and he would play the latest tune he had composed for a particular poem, and would let me make suggestions. But there is a slight difference in writing for fun and doing them to order. And as the previous work had just been written for fun, I found it much harder to do thirty or forty more poems for the second book. But nevertheless, I burnt a lot of midnight oil, or indeed candles, and finally came up with the required amount. Once again, we went into a recording studio, and this time I was allowed to appear on the album and we were joined by Noel Edmonds. By now the company who had bought the rights decided that 'Captain Beaky' should be made into bedspreads, wallpaper, toys and mugs. There would be Hissing Sid snakes as door-stops.

All these things appeared, but as so often happens in these instances, not in time. Although the second LP and the second book were successful, by the time these items got to the market, the fever had rather disappeared. I still have a great number of rolls of wallpaper, slippers, one or two mugs, a few Hissing Sid doorstops, and some rather bad hearth rugs, all with the 'Beaky' designs on them. One of the LPs was also translated into Swedish; it makes fascinating listening. I remember at the time 'Captain Beaky' was such a cult, a lot of political cartoons appeared depicting the Cabinet of the day as the various animals in the story. Such was the effect of the characters that the police had to search for a small boy who had run away from home to look for Captain Beaky and his Band, so he could live like them in the woods. Fortunately, they found him. But it is nice to have created characters who can set fire to the imagination in such a dramatic way. I still bump into people who can remember naming their animals or friends 'Hissing Sid', 'Timid Toad', or 'Reckless Rat' – there was even a horse I believe called 'Captain Beaky'. There was certainly a boat called 'Captain Beaky', I saw it in the South of France. I don't expect to go down in history for this, but it is nice to have made a slight dent in that brief fifteen minutes of fame that Andy Warhol was always going on about.

I also wrote a 'Captain Beaky' pantomime, which was put on at the Gate Theatre, Chester. It was one of the best evenings that I can remember. Sitting in a small theatre, absolutely crammed with children, screaming and shouting with excitement as Captain Beaky and his Band marched from poem to poem, meeting such adversaries as 'Ida the Spider', 'The Great Hairy Navin of Nairn', before losing themselves on the great Mcsponge moor, as they attempted to return 'Dilys the Dachshund' back to her normal form, after she had been changed into a bumble bee by a witch. A normal day in the life of characters that children can relate to.

I remember being as excited as any of the small children as I sat on the front row and Captain Beaky picked up a plastic bucket and reaching down into Harold the Lonely Frog's reflecting pool, scooped up what we all assumed was water and threw a bucketful of confetti over us. I roared with delight just like the rest. I realized I hadn't grown up at all. And why should I? I was having too good a time.

It was directed by Miss Nona Shepherd and is still available should anyone wish to do it. What a pity so many people can't lend themselves to the world of illusion today. That is to say the world of charming illusion. I don't mean the world where people can get hit by realistic blood-bullets; or get blown through windows or out of cars. Every time I turn on the television it would seem to me that the world has become more violent. Particularly the world of film. Unless somebody is dying, crashing or being blown up, it doesn't have much chance of getting on, unless it's a comedy. The most violent of all are the children's video games, but I suppose thinking back, roasting small boys in front of the fire, or putting plasters on popping out brains or jumping on someone's glass eye wouldn't make a very good television show either. So I suppose from the child's point of view it all seems perfectly normal. But I do notice that Cox's Pippin apples don't taste quite as good as they used to. Flowers don't have quite the same smell either, but that's probably because I smoke. And I don't recall having seen a rainbow for quite a long time.

A musical was planned too. I was in the music business in a big way. The BBC made two fifty-minute specials, featuring most of the artists on the record: Harry Secombe, Gordon Jackson, Petula Clarke, Noel Edmonds, Penelope Keith, Peter Skellern, myself and of course Keith Michell, who again did all the lovely drawings. In fact all except dear Peter Sellers, who had died by then. Harry Secombe was marvellous declaiming the 'Saga of Harold the Lonely Frog', who was shunned by other frogs because he had a wet and boggy smell; Penelope Keith did 'Dilys the Dachshund', who wanted to be a ballerina and was very good at doing a *paw de deux*, Gordon Jackson sang the 'Saga of the Haggis and the Great Hairy Navin of Nairn' and Noel Edmonds was quite hysterical recounting the birth of a cuckoo in a straw hat while it was on the head of a tramp. I settled for 'Wendle the Worm', which didn't know one end from the other.

We got about nine million viewers which is fairly amazing

for BBC 2. This naturally put the book sales up enormously. I was quite sure I'd be able to retire, perhaps to Stoke Court. I should have read the contract more closely: it wasn't a very good deal I had signed. I do remember seeing one account, saying £20 000 had been received by the Beaky Company; my share was £300. But then who was I to complain? I had had a success in another medium; I had done well at school. Are you listening Daddy? Grandma? Margo Lees? Damn, why didn't they wait?

Early in 1980 the musical appeared. It even got a good review from Jack Tinker. I say that because he doesn't seem to like a lot. *The Times* called it 'an evening of enchantment'. It was a small cast: Keith Michell, Eleanor Bron, Twiggy, and myself. Accompanied by a small orchestra, we recounted the 'Tango of the Gypsy Moths', and the 'Captain Beaky Saga', with a solo from Twiggy about the plight of a Cockney Sparrow. The audience called for encore after encore, I think we did most of the show twice. It was a riot. If you were there, you would remember it. I'll remember it for always. It would have been a good night to die, but fate had a couple of minor tasks left for me.

Unknown to me in the audience on the last night was a canon of the Church of England, the Reverend Peter Delaney. He came with a group of rather tough school kids who enjoyed it. I bumped into him some time later, when he was having dinner with Liza Minnelli and her husband. He had married them in America where afterwards they had entertained him at the Tramp Nightclub – not a place you would expect to meet a gentleman of the cloth. We got chatting which wasn't difficult as I'd met Liza Minnelli before in America. In fact, I seemed to have met most of America when I was there.

The Reverend Delaney thought I had got a very good way of putting things over to kids and wondered if I could have a go at making the Bible easier to understand for children. I readily agreed. I wasn't sure how serious he was, but after my twelve times table and making gun powder, I had actually been rather good at religion, not because I was over-zealously religious, but because of the adventures: like the Plague; the parting of the Red Sea, and the Walls of Jericho blowing down. These stories had always seemed rather exciting. I decided to give it my best effort, and thought I'd better hurry as I hadn't been feeling too well, having been a short time before rushed to the London Clinic when some of the plumbing had gone wrong. (An ulcer had burst and I had had a haemorrhage. It's always an exciting thing to have at night, when you are living alone. Lots of blood and all you can get is the doctor's answering machine.) So I did think if I was going to do anything worthwhile I had better do it now, before something else went that even a medical Shrapnel Smith couldn't repair. So I sat down and wrote a children's version of the New Testament, as told by Captain Beaky and his Band. I remember driving down to All Hallows by the Tower of London, which was the Reverend Delaney's church in the city of London and dropping the manuscript in the letter box with a note saying: 'If there's any of this that's worth using, please have it with my best compliments.'

As you can imagine I was very surprised when I received a letter from him, saying that the Archbishop of Canterbury had enjoyed it enormously and was prepared to write a foreword to the book. I hadn't even planned a book. I took the letter and a copy of the manuscript and gave it to my agent. Within a week, Faber and Faber had agreed to publish and I received a cheque. Such was the popularity caused by the previous exposure to the world of Captain Beaky and his Band, that the *Woodland Gospels* became a bestseller as well. By now I was waiting to be made at least Dean of St Paul's, but somehow I was overlooked.

America also took to the book and in the American version it was foreworded by most of the denominations from Catholic to Baptist. In fact, I did a book tour in America for Faber and Faber; from Los Angeles to St Louis. Whenever I did radio shows with phone-ins, most of the questions were about my life on *Laugh In*. It had obviously left a deep impression on the general public. I must say seeing parts of America, other than Los Angeles and New York, was quite an experience. I was in Chicago, Denver and Dallas, and even managed to attend a polo match in Houston, in which a friend of mine, Stephanie Powers was playing. I was given a lift back to Los Angeles in the Texan Oilers Football Team's private jet. The guardian angel was working overtime. I was interviewed on the *Merv Griffin Show*. I mentioned that I had been a temporary rat-catcher and he said that in America cats do that sort of thing. He got a lot of laughs at my expense, and I got twenty minutes on his show.

During the tour, the *Woodland Gospels* came to the attention of my dear friend, Mr Herman Rush, still President of Columbia Television. He considered this was an ideal subject for his company to make and the Dic Cartoon Company was employed to do the drawings, whilst I was flown to New York to meet the head of the World Council of Churches to discuss the important things: like, am I allowed to say it was an apple on the tree in the Garden of Eden or should it be a plum? The World Council of Churches considered this question carefully; the religious advisor/producer who had been brought in by Mr Rush needed confirmation on such important details. The head of the World Council of Churches happened to be a lady called Dr Joan. Dr Joan considered the point carefully and said I could indeed use an apple. Although it wasn't specified in the Bible what fruit it had been. Funny, I always thought it had been an apple. Certainly in the great drawings it had always been an apple. The religious advisor asked Dr Joan if she would assist the television company to promote this wonderful work in all pre-school church groups. She readily agreed. I was very pleased.

I then hit a number of unexpected problems. The religious advisor, I'm not quite sure what religion he was, insisted on vetting every story. I got through the Garden of Eden quite well, though Adam was not allowed to be white or black. Adam was portrayed as a shadow, so there would be no argument. I didn't own the rights to Captain Beaky and his Band, so I changed the names to Professor Pelican and his Friends: a lady toad; two mice, who were children; a chameleon called Clarence to provide the comedy, and the whole thing was to be done as a cartoon. I was flown back to New York to meet the man who was going to do the music, a wonderful man called Joe Reposo, who had done all the music and songs for *Sesame Street*, the most memorable of which I remember is Kermit sitting on some stairs singing 'I am green'. Joe Reposo was a plump jolly man, with a great sense of humour, who wrote the music for the title song of the show, which was now called *The Bible Explorers*, plus the music for the other songs, the lyrics of which I had already written. He had a splendid office over Carnegie Hall and I was very pleased to have worked with him. Sadly, he died in his early forties, before the show was made.

Back in Hollywood I worked away on the Bible stories and attended regular meetings with the cartoon company. The actual drawings were done in Singapore and Hong Kong, but the basic sketches were drawn in detailed perspectives, before they were sent to the Orient to be drawn properly. My main problem was the religious advisor/producer, who kept arguing every theological point possible. If I was doing the story about the Flood, I must mention other floods at the time. I had never heard of other floods; there was only one flood as far a I was concerned and Noah's Ark was in the middle of it. I had my characters stranded on a raft left behind by the Flood. This is difficult said the advisor; in the Bible, every animal is on the Ark. I know I said, but I am writing a children's version of this. These are our heroes; they were swept back in time on a raft and they are back in the Flood and they are not on the Ark. This argument carried on for a week. Calls were made to the Head of the World Council of Churches; apparently it was all right to have my animals on a raft. They were visiting the scene like reporters.

The next problem was Jonah and the Whale; this was an almost insurmountable problem. The religious advisor told me that there had been a leviathan lurking in the sea in some versions of the Bible. So I should mention the leviathan. I had never heard of the leviathan; I just wanted to mention Jonah and the Whale plus Professor Pelican and his friends, who were also swallowed by the whale, so they could have a chat with Jonah. The leviathan problem held us up for quite a long time. Finally I was allowed not to have the leviathan, but by then I had written three stories involving it. The leviathan had been drawn by the cartoon company, and the whole thing was costing rather a lot of money.

The Plagues of Egypt were another problem. I was now supposed to write about plagues that weren't too frightening for children. I had to substitute measles or chicken pox. A difficult theological problem to solve. I was writing six or seven versions of each biblical story; the cartoonists were drawing furiously.

I returned to England in the middle of all of this to deal with some more writing at home. David Croft noticed I had one or two grey hairs which were a surprise to me as I thought I had the secret of eternal youth. I decided to have my hair lightened slightly. Unfortunately, the particular hairdresser was busy talking to another customer as he put a preparation on my head. By that evening I found that I had green hair. I'd just made the startling discovery when I got a phone call at about midnight from Herman Rush in Hollywood.

'Hi, Jeremy. We've got people who are auditioning for the voices of Professor Pelican and his gang. Hold the phone! We've got a great guy for Miss Toad.'

'Hello,' croaked a voice, 'I'm auditioning for the Frog.'

'It's a lady toad,' I said.

'OK,' said the croaky voice and he began.

'As he croaked away in my ear, I made a mental note that I was probably the only person in London with green hair, listening to a man imitating a lady toad. I listened to some

Clarence the Chameleons, a number of Professor Pelicans, and some very squeaky Mice Children before going to sleep. I went back to the hairdresser's and had my hair returned to something near normal, although not quite. Gorden Kaye made the best remark: 'Isn't that the colour hair goes after grey?' Nice one Gorden!

When I got back to America and *The Bible Explorers*, the first cartoon was ready. I thought it was jolly good. Thirty-four more were planned, but then Columbia was taken over by a Japanese company and Herman Rush retired. The pilot was shelved and Professor Pelican died a natural death, together with his companions. Once again, I had failed. *Nil desperandum* (perfect Latin, thanks to a Dunwell beating!).

10

As *Are You Being Served?* had finished, David Croft was looking for another show. I suggested something to do with the French Resistance, and on that slim premise we sat down and created *'Allo 'Allo*. It was successful from the word 'go', although some of the reviews were rather mixed with some people taking exception to our making fun of the War. In fact, we had no intention of upsetting anybody; there had been plenty of films, in which both the First and Second World Wars had been used as a basis for comedy, stretching back to the days of *The Great Dictator*, starring Charlie Chaplin. Despite the controversy, the show gained an enormous audience and started to be shown around the world, even in countries that had been very heavily occupied, such as Denmark and France.

Once again, David chose the cast. The star, Gorden Kaye, had already appeared in a couple of *Are You Being Served?* shows, and another short series we'd written for Harry Worth called *Oh, Happy Band*. And I must say, Gorden Kaye was an ideal choice. Filming is always great fun. We used to spend about three weeks filming the exteriors, and as you can imagine, with a cast like that, there is really never a dull moment. Although it was quite an expensive show to make, with the comparatively large cast. However, I think the overseas sales probably justified its costs. And now the ninetieth show has just been written. David gave up about twenty-six shows ago to concentrate on *You Rang M'Lord*, and I was lucky enough to find a writing partner called Paul Adam, who was rather like me when I started at the Grafton Arms: keen and for whom nothing is too much trouble. He has a great sense of humour, and hopefully has learnt quite a lot from the experience, as it is his first show. I wish him well.

Sadly during the course of the series we lost dear old Jack Haig, who played Monsieur Leclerc. Needless to say, he had the last laugh at the crematorium: the music he chose was 'Smoke Gets in Your Eyes'. It's very hard to cry and laugh at the same time, but I think we all managed it.

As devotees of this show will know, it also became a very successful stage play, hated by the critics, but loved by the public. In fact, it brought people into the theatre, who had never ever been before. I remember on one of the opening tour nights, going to the Liverpool Empire, which has three thousand seats – it is an enormous theatre – and there were queues round the block and the Liverpudlian usherettes were dressed as can-can dancers, and thoroughly enjoying themselves, as they showed people to their seats, with the words: 'This way, *s'il vous plait*.' On some of the tour dates, some of the audience would appear dressed in British, French or German uniforms and imitate the characters. This really had a far bigger success than I had ever imagined when we wrote the first one in my cottage in St James's.

Whose idea was the policeman, who spoke bad French? I must admit it was David Croft's. I've got a lot to thank him for and do.

Recently *Are You Being Served?* was revived in a new form, or sequel; my turn for a good idea. The characters have now moved into a country house called Millstone Manor, and it is entitled *Grace and Favour*, although in America, it is called *Are You Being Served Again?*, which I think is a much better title, and so does David.

It was so nice to be reunited with old friends. Show business friendships can often be very transient – enthusiastic meetings, a lot of hugging and kissing on the cheek: 'Darling, must meet again as soon as possible,' (this greeting I use for girls) – then nothing until the next time we happen to meet, either on a film set or in some television show. That's not to say I don't consider the cast of *Are You Being Served?* my friends, as I'm sure they do me. And after spending nine or ten years with them and another ten years with the cast of *'Allo 'Allo*, we have all got to know each other very well. But this doesn't mean that we meet each other socially. The most social event is the post production party, which is usually held in a room at the BBC, after shooting the last show of a particular series. And where I am always surprised that actors and actresses actually have wives and husbands, and when not playing their parts lead quite a normal life.

Naturally we are all on call for each other, should there ever be an emergency. Such as the terrible time when Gorden Kaye had that most unfortunate accident, sitting in his car in the height of a gale, when a wooden hoarding broke through the window and impaled itself on his head. I was making a cup of tea in the kitchen, and heard it on the six o'clock news. I rushed to the hospital. Needless to say, the papers were there like vultures. One reporter from the tabloid press, I believe, even posed as a doctor and tried to get into the room to photograph the unfortunate Gorden. I sat by Gorden's bedside as he lay unconscious, connected to tubes. I remember how helpless I felt and all I could do was talk to him, hoping he might hear me. Hoping it might strike a chord, I mentioned that the show, which was on at the Palladium, would be transferring to Australia in about a week and if he didn't recover, he wouldn't be able to go. Unfortunately, he was too unconscious even to react. I believe part of his recovery was due to his agent getting a video and showing reruns of *'Allo 'Allo* to remind him who he was.

To the relief of everybody, Gorden made a remarkable recovery, but still has no recollection of the accident. I must say as I write about this, I am looking forward even more eagerly to working again with the cast of both *'Allo 'Allo* and *Grace and Favour.* Both casts are rather like a family you don't see very often.

An average day at the start of a new series goes something like this. First we have a read-through. The cast gather round a big table in a rehearsal room in Acton, known at the BBC as the Acton Hilton and if it happens to be *'Allo 'Allo*, we can be sure that Richard Gibson will be late, that Vicki Michelle will just make it, and Carmen Silvera will be doing a crossword right up to the moment the director, the erstwhile John Hobbs, raps on the table and calls for silence. This is always ignored, and chattering only stops when Gorden Kaye launches into his opening speech. Nobody would dream of making a bad career move by interrupting him. The writers sit back and try to look nonchalant, while straining to hear the slightest laugh. And the cast, who have become fairly immured over the years to other actors' jokes, wait their turn to be funny. Nevertheless, it usually turns out to be a very good humoured experience, until we find the show is too long, then I find myself frantically cutting bits out as they rehearse the opening scene. By the end of the day the whole thing is about the right length and it has got four or five new jokes in. The worst thing is trying to take somebody's joke out.

'I like that joke,' an actor will say. 'It's probably the best joke I've got, you can't take that joke out.' If you do take it out, you have to put another one in to satisfy them. Richard Marner, who plays Colonel Von Strom, is always very keen to have more jokes, but he also complains that the scripts are different each week and he has to learn new ones. It never ceases to amaze me how Arthur Bostrom, who plays the English agent posing as a policeman, manages to speak his bad French so fluently. Although we write it phonetically, he always makes it sound even funnier. And he's almost word perfect even before the read-through. I suppose with that tricky sort of language you have got to know it pretty well, otherwise it is very easy to make a mistook, I mean mistake.

The most dedicated actor in the whole cast, I think, is Rose Hill, who plays Madame Fanny; she draws musical notes over her dialogue, indicating cadences where her voice should rise and fall. Naturally, she gives a brilliant performance every time, and only becomes temperamental when she has to deal with special effects, such as her hair standing on end due to an electric shock, when the secret radio short circuits through her bedstead. I'm sure even Vanessa Redgrave would get a bit tricky, if her hair didn't stand up at the right time in similar circumstances.

Richard Gibson of course is excellent as the smooth-haired, steel-rimmed, bespectacled Herr Flick and we are lucky to have him at all, because he is very talented in other directions – acting not being his only career, as he is also involved in the world of production, and obviously has quite a future in that direction. Just a titbit of information: few people know that Guy Siner is half American. Guy, of course, is the excellent Lieutenant Gruber, a slightly camp German, who is one of Rene's greatest admirers, in the plot that is. Guy is a very thoughtful actor, usually to be seen smoking a small cigar as he acquaints himself with the latest script, often calling me aside to point out a slight error that I might have made, such as not building his character up as much as I might. I hasten to add this is all done very good humouredly.

Rehearsals last from about ten-thirty in the morning till two or three in the afternoon, with a break for lunch in the canteen on the top floor. Richard Gibson has a mischievous sense of humour and often makes alterations to the main menu at the doorway, adding fried weasel or baked terrapin, which I'm sure dissuades one or two from sitting down at all. It's quite difficult sometimes dealing with a comedy cast, particularly when we were working at Elstree making the show where we had a set of the village square. This was in the same studio block as *EastEnders*, and in one of the pub scenes in that famous series, some members of the cast of *'Allo 'Allo* managed to infiltrate themselves into the crowd. The director, not being familiar with *'Allo 'Allo* merely thought there were many extras and filmed the scene. It was only later that it was realized that faces from another series could be clearly seen. I'm sure Richard Gibson was behind that as well.

Kenneth Connor who plays Monsieur Alfonse, the under-taker, is of course a wonderful comedian of the old school. He has had tremendous success for years, appearing in many *Carry On* films, if not all of them, and he is a brilliant raconteur. Quite often interrupting proceedings when other people are rehearsing, as his small group of listeners bursts into laughter, which results in a lot of ssh-ing from the director. The whole thing is slightly reminiscent of being at school, except that some of the pupils are in their late seventies.

Once the cast gets into the studio to rehearse with the cameras, it becomes quite a serious business again. I think the remarks in the control room would make a show in themselves: 'What's that idiot doing in my shot? Does the electrician have to be in every scene I shoot? Where's the wig? I thought Rose was supposed to be wearing a wig. Get the floor manager. Where's Rose's wig?'

'It's in hairdressing.'

'What's it doing in hairdressing? It's supposed to be on her head. This is a technical run-through.'

'She says she'll mime the wig.'

'She can't mime the wig, it's supposed to stand up when she gets electrified.'

'The wig's on its way!'

'Good.'

'Hairdressing are just giving it a final brush.'

'We can't hold up this whole show for hairdressing.'

'The wig is here!'

'Well get her to put it on.'

'She wants to say something.'

'Get a microphone near her. Yes Rose, this is John, what is it?'

'I've got the wig.'

'Yes, we can see that; it's on television and we've got screens up here. So we can see what's going on, but I don't like the look of that wig. That's not the wig we used in rehearsal. Where's the stage manager?'

'I'm on headphones, can you hear me, John?'

'Yes, that's not the wig we used in rehearsal.'

'No, it's a wig we got from hairdressing.'

'That wig looks far too good. Where's the one we used in rehearsal?'

'It's in hairdressing.'

'Good God, we're never going to get this show made. Go and get it.'

'Rose wants to speak to you.'

'Yes, Rose, can you hear me?'

'Yes. I want to wear *this* wig.'

'You can't, it doesn't look funny.'

'It's a better fit than the other one.'

'I don't mind how good the fit is, Rose, this one doesn't look funny. The other one does.'

'What's the difference?'

'At the moment about ten minutes.'

'The other one was very moth-eaten.'

'Yes, that's what we liked about it.'

'Hello, John can you hear me?'

'Yes.'

'We've got the other wig.'

'Well take that unfunny wig off and put the funny one on.'

'Rose wants to keep the first one.'

'She *can't* keep the first one. Look, I'm losing time here. Just take the old wig and give her the new wig. Tell her we're about to start the scene. Can they hear me down there?'

'No, John.'

'I've had more trouble with that wig than I've had with the

whole script. And what's that? What's that electrician doing in the bedroom? That man gets in every scene. Tell him to get out of the shot. What's he doing? Trying for an Equity card?'

'He's out of shot, John!'

'Right, let's go!'

'Can you hear me John?'

'Yes, what is it?'

'Sound's got a problem. The boom's broken down, and they can't get it over Rose.'

'Get a fishing rod and dangle a microphone near her. We've got to get this shot.'

'John, can you hear me?'

'Yes, what is it now?'

'It's Monsieur Leclerc, he's been under the bedcovers and he's suffocating, can he come up for air?'

'Of course, he can. Got the fishing rod?'

'Yes. Are we ready to go?'

'Yes.'

'Thank goodness. I could have done the chariot race from *Ben Hur* in this time. Action!'

During all this the writers have been sitting, looking relaxed. This is beyond anything they can do to help, this is in the high realms of show business. Our main objective is to try and get to the bag of sweets next to the director without him noticing. By the end of the run-through, though, all the problems had been ironed out. Well, as far as possible, all technical difficulties are overcome. All that remains is to call the cast to sit in the seats that will be shortly occupied by the audience to receive a lecture on how bad they were, how much more zip they've got to put into it, and a reminder to some of them to try and say some of the lines that were in the script. It's amazing how the actual show galvanizes everybody into action.

A packed audience breathlessly await the appearance of their heroes; the floor manager announces a comedian who will entertain them in the breaks between the scenes. It is quite often Felix Burness; he has a stuttering delivery which keeps them very amused. He introduces Gorden Kaye, who gets a big round of applause, and then Gorden introduces the rest of the cast, usually with very pithy comments on the side, delivered in Franglais. Silence is called for and the show gets on the way. The fear of the occasion usually produces the best performances of the week.

The show takes about an hour and a half to make. Afterwards, everybody is absolutely exhausted. The writers go round with the producer and director, knocking on the doors. Exhausted actors in dressing gowns appear to ask if it was all okay? I don't think the public realize how much actors put into the job, and how much they give of themselves. But I can tell you they work very hard indeed. It would be unfair of me not to mention that Vicki Michelle and Sue Hodge do a lot to keep everybody's morale up. Particularly the writers'. The more I think about it, I am very very sorry that the last of this series is about to be filmed, and I shall miss it a lot. Fortunately, it will continue circulating around the world. No doubt one day I'll be a tax exile in Bolivia and the cast will appear on the screen with subtitles and I will remember the day at the studio when that show was actually made and regret that one or two of the better jokes had to be cut out, because the show had been too long. But as Crabtree the policeman would say: 'It's a gid loof, if you don't wicken.'

It's extraordinary to think that in the last twenty-two years, *Are You Being Served?* and *'Allo 'Allo* formed the major part of my writing life. Well, I suppose I should include 'Captain Beaky' in that as well. I'm sure I've missed out quite a lot of things that have happened, but then so much has happened it's very hard to remember everything. I have never been very good at keeping memorabilia, but as I look round myself, I can see the fickle finger of fate from *Laugh In*; a rather faded photograph of me in an Air Force uniform with Leslie Phillips from

A Very Important Person; a mug from the 'Captain Beaky' days, with Hissing Sid curled round the handle; a photograph of *Captain Beaky* at the Lyric Theatre, with my name in lights, and I notice that I appear to have been in *The Four Musketeers* at Drury Lane, which I haven't even mentioned at all, though I seem to remember being in it for about two years. It starred Harry Secombe and was just a lot of fun. Oh yes, I also have the tape of the *Eve Arden Special* I did, and a rather faded cheque from the late 1960s, paid out by a gambling club in London, but hardly worth mentioning because I spent it so quickly.

While writing this book, I have had a moment to reflect on my life. It all seems to have passed rather quickly. A cousin of mine once said, just before he relinquished his mortal coil, 'Good heavens, I've only just arrived and here I am going.' I feel the same, except I don't intend to depart just yet. I'm sure there's still lots to do; though having a normal family life does seem to have eluded me. I did get engaged during the run of *'Allo 'Allo* to Carole Ashby, who plays the demented Louise of the Communist Resistance. Although now disengaged we remain good friends. I think we were attracted to each other because of our very similar backgrounds – she too came from Didsbury. In fact, we went back there trying to find the houses we had lived in. I am afraid it had all changed, and we hardly recognized anything. Carole now lives in America, where she is pursuing her career, but she still pops back to play Louise. And as a single girl, in Hollywood she is very popular. I know, because she sends reports home.

Mind you, Far Eastern countries' advertisements for single men and women use up a great deal of this planet's forestry resources, I remember reading one such advertisement some years ago in my local paper: 'Natural blonde, thirty-five, enjoys badminton, reading, cricket, horse riding, sailing, classical music, bridge, cooking, walking and the theatre. Seeks man with same interests.' It is immediately evident to the single male that the upkeep of these activities would seem to give this advertiser little time for housework, or even light dusting.

Shortly after reading it, a phone call invited me to a dinner party, given by married friends; the wife confided that the dinner was to introduce me to a darling girl, who was too sweet, and only in her late twenties.

'Did you tell her my age?'

'She would never believe it, darling. You don't look anything like it.'

It's not surprising as I still do three hundred and sixty-five press-ups a year. I slipped into one of my best suits and found a pair of socks that nearly matched. I looked at the result in my bathroom mirror and found myself looking at my father, whom I had begun to vaguely resemble. I wondered if I should forget the whole thing, but thought I might as well give it a go. I arrived on the doorstep in a state of slight euphoria, due to the fact that I had found the missing matching sock in the sleeve of my coat. I rang the bell and kissed my hostess on both cheeks, as is the local custom, and shook her husband's hand. Removing my ex-Russian cavalry fur-lined, ankle-length great coat, I placed it over the outstretched arm of a very thin woman in black, who like all good servants had appeared silently beside me. As has happened before, the recipient of the coat obviously misjudged it's weight and fell back at an angle of forty-five degrees and vanished into the dining room, accompanied by a crash of breaking glass.

'Where is my dream date?' I said. The hostess explained I had just handed my coat to her. It took almost two courses, and all the charm of any character I might have invented, before my date thawed out. By the time the port had travelled round the table, she looked positively radiant and laughed a lot with me, at my amusing remarks. I began to think: why fight this? I can't be alone forever. This charming lady is as pretty as a picture, very well dressed and, judging by the photos of the children, they would soon be old enough to keep us, should we fall on hard times.

'Tell me,' I said, 'what sort of things would you like to share with a rather demented writer with his own teeth, who is actually seven years older than he's just admitted?'

The perfect mate did not pause. She'd like to share her love of badminton, reading, cricket, horse riding, sailing, classical music, bridge, cooking, walking and the theatre. I wondered if I would ever have time for writing and decided that being alone was probably the best answer.

Looking back over the formative years of no talent, and arriving at the stage where I have a roof over my head and am of reasonably independent means is really an achievement that my father in his wildest moments could never have imagined. As I mentioned earlier, my life had been briefly mapped out when I was very young by a crystal ball gazing lady, whose forecasts have been uncannily accurate. This was not my only brush with the supernatural, which is a subject that has always been of great interest to me. I have seen some of the best crystal ball gazers, hand readers, tarot card readers, spiritualists and most psychics known to mankind, though some are now in the past tense.

I remember arriving in Singapore for an overnight stay before I went on to Australia to do the *Are You Being Served?* series, and by chance meeting a certain Professor Bennett, a palmist to world leaders. He let me look through his correspondence. Everyone seemed to have sent him an imprint of their palm. I remember looking at President Nixon's, attached was a copy of Professor Bennett's letter, warning him that he was going to have a lot of problems in the White House. This was before Watergate. I was fascinated to hear what the future held for me. I gave him my hand, he made an ink imprint on paper and I sat anxiously, while he consulted charts of the solar system together with his own book on hands. To my relief he saw a longer life than the one previously promised and also a great success; he stabbed his finger on a map of the solar system, consulted his book, did some arithmetic and announced confidently that I would go down in history. Unfortunately, he didn't say what as. Up to now, of course, I hadn't revealed my occupation, but asked him if I should ever write and tell him if history made a note of my existence. He assured me that he was in touch with the outside world and he would be bound to hear of it. I am still waiting to go down in history. I hope it's not in something like the *Titanic*.

I also saw a very famous psychic in Los Angeles. A world-renowned Dutchman. He got very excited about my hand. He saw a lot of money. He saw so much he tried to sell me some land that he owned, which he assured me had natural gas deposits buried beneath it. I said I thought I should wait until the money actually arrived before we discussed any business propositions. He also mentioned that I would be on an aeroplane travelling over an uncharted jungle and the plane would crash and I would be the sole survivor. I would be rescued by a forgotten tribe and be missing from the outside world for some time. This of course tied up with Professor Bennett's prediction that I would go down in history. No doubt, when I was discovered, which the Dutch seer said I would be eventually, the forgotten tribe would be discovered at the same time and I would have been partly responsible for bringing them to light. He saw something like a Dakota, the first three registration letters being G.A.Y. This was slightly worrying, but after consulting his crystal-ball more closely, he changed the Y to an X. He gave such a vivid description of my escape, and the search that was to take place, that I was quite sure I must have done something rather special to deserve it. Normally one would expect a headline like: 'Writer vanishes in jungle; David Croft takes on new partner'. Needless to say, I am still awaiting this disappearance.

I had another interesting psychic experience on Brighton seafront once. There was a row of huts down near the beach not far from the pier, and on the door of one of them was a notice proclaiming that Madame X could, for the sum of ten shillings, take on the shape and appearance of any departed famous person and it invited callers to knock. I had driven down from London just to have a crunch on the pebbles and look at the sea and breathe in a bit of industrial waste and so I duly knocked. I was invited in. Madame X was a rather large woman and proudly showed me a newspaper cutting, indicating that a television company had been down to film this phenomenon. The headline read: 'Remarkable Transfiguration in Brighton'. The cutting informed me that Madame X had summoned up many characters from the past, and the correspondent had called it unbelievable! Madame X took this to be a compliment; 'Yah,' she said. ''E couldn't believe it. All I do is take a deep breath and concentrate with the name firmly fixed in my subconscious. Who would you like?'

I paused, thinking who I would like to see. She helped me and suggested Churchill. He was available at the moment. I paid ten shillings and waited for Churchill to arrive. Madame X took some very deep breaths, sat back and shuddered a lot, and then words sprang out of the corner of her mouth: ''E's 'ere.' She sat up, with her neck muscles bulging and her head sunk down into her chest and said in a deep Churchillian voice: 'Give us the tools and we'll do the job.' She collapsed limply after this impressive demonstration, breathing heavily.

I said, 'It's unbelievable.'

'That's what they all say,' she said. 'I can contact Jesus, but 'e's a quid.'

I waved my hand dismissively, no. I assured her he was probably very busy with more important things.

'Then 'ow about Jayne Mansfield?'

I remembered that Jayne had had a rather unfortunate demise, being decapitated in a car, and tried to think of someone before she could take another deep breath. 'Here's somebody really famous,' I said. 'How about Plato?'

Without pause, she said: 'That'll be Walt Disney, dear and 'e's always very busy.'

At that moment we were interrupted by a stone hitting the door, followed by a few more bangs as stones rained on the door. ''Em blasted boys, 'ang on.' She went to the door, obscuring most of the doorway and I noticed she took a deep breath and stood there, the sound of running feet disappeared into the distance. She came back. 'I called up 'Itler. That always scares 'em. Now where was we?' It cost me another thirty shillings: Mae West – 'Come up and see me sometime'; Queen Victoria – 'we was not amused' and I then had a brief meeting with my great-great-grandmother who was apparently called Rosie and lived in Paris and drank a lot. No remaining member of my family has been able to verify this, but her opening words of ''Ello stranger', indicated that she had not been paying much attention to me from her position in the heavenly realms. Needless to say, I took none of this seriously, but it certainly provided an entertaining moment on an otherwise rather boring day at the end of the summer. I must add that, rather more frighteningly, real events of the supernatural have indeed occurred to me.

For instance, although divorced from Joanna Lumley, we still remained very good friends. I remember one night retiring to bed, after a hot bath, in my flat only a few miles from where she lived. I had just put my head on the pillow, when I heard what I can only describe as a vibrating noise and I suddenly had an extraordinary sensation that I was being swept out of my body and I remember putting my hands up to deflect the impact as I flew through the wall. Then in what seemed like only a moment I found myself standing in Joanna's bedroom. Not a bad shot, come to think of it! I was aware that I was still the same height, but had a consistency of grey jelly, and that also my feet weren't actually on the floor, but two or three inches below. The room was unoccupied, but I could hear her talking to a friend in her living room. By leaning forward, I managed to half-float and half-walk in the direction of the voices and, arriving at the doorway, I observed Joanna and her friend having a conversation. It was about two o'clock in the morning. I recognized the girl she was talking to as an actress with whom we had both worked. I tried to speak, but found I couldn't. The effort cost me any remaining energy I might have had and I found myself flying back through the wall of my room, back into my body, where my head was still on the pillow. It had been so remarkably clear that I sat up and telephoned immediately.

'Hello.'

'Hello, J.L. What are you doing phoning at this time?'

'Well, I've just been over there.'

'What? What do you mean?'

I reported the conversation I had heard. There was silence at the other end for a moment. I was told not to do it again. I never did. But I did have a call from Joanna one day to say that I had materialized in her living room, holding up a news-paper – I think it was *The Times* – and pointing to my obituary. She was quite concerned. Was I all right?

'Yes, I'm absolutely fine. Was it a big obituary?'

'Yes.'

'Which page? What was I wearing at the time, did it mention the lost tribe?'

'No,' said Joanna. 'I just called to make sure you were all right.' And I was.

Since then I have had a number of experiences where I seemed to have jumped out of my body and visited friends. One even called me from Africa to say that I had appeared suddenly and disappeared again. Was I all right? Yes, I was fine. It's quite clear that I have a lot of extra-curricular activity at night. Sometimes I remember it, sometimes I don't.

The most frightening experience was zooming back through the wall one night, and arriving back in bed aware that I had been somewhere, but with no idea of where. As I lay there, trying to remember, I heard some very heavy breathing about a foot away. Somebody else was in bed with me. This was rather unnerving as I was living alone at the time.

'Good heavens! I've brought something back with me. Some being from beyond.' It sounded like a man breathing. I reached for the bedside table to get some leverage, so I could leap out and run for the door. To my surprise my arm, which seemed perfectly solid to me, went straight through the table and at that instant I shot across the bed and arrived in the recumbent breathing form, only to find it was me who was breathing heavily. I could not reach the table from where I was, and realized that I had had a psychic experience, which had left my heart beating rather rapidly.

Since then I don't seem to have had any out-of-the-body experiences, which is just as well. Though reading books afterwards, it seemed that this was not an entirely uncommon occurrence. Whether there's life after death is always something that's intrigued me. But life as a grey sort of jelly doesn't sound a lot of fun. And yet again there's the problem of companionship. Most of the people I like are still here; I don't imagine I would get on better with my father in the after life than I did in this one. Certainly my mother and I would have a bit of catching up to do. I'd be pleased to see my grandmother and listen once more to how the Zeppelin was shot down over Ilford. And hopefully I'd be reunited with Ostrich, the grey ex-race horse which I used to gallop along the banks of the Thames, accompanied by Jock the faithful sheepdog, whom I've not mentioned before. But he's probably better remembered by me than a lot of people I've had dinner with. But I must say I certainly hope there is something.

I had some very expensive dental work done recently as well and it would be a shame to leave all that behind to find there was nothing, particularly if I haven't had a chance to amortize it. But who knows? Perhaps one of you readers may come across a very aged Madame X, possibly semi-retired in a caravan. I may have gone down in history and she may call upon a famous person. You could possibly hear the startling words: 'I'm free,' or ''allo, 'allo', and wonder who the hell was that? Unless of course you happened to be a fan of either show. If I do come back at all, I would rather like to be a giant turtle; they live way over a hundred years, are free to travel and always have a roof over their heads. I must send a subscription off to Greenpeace.

I'm sure Doctor Dunwell would also have approved of my

interest in wild animals and the preservation of rare species. This interest recently brought me into contact with a young beautiful lion tamer, Collette Northtrop. She brought a wild panther to our wedding in Palm Beach, Florida, and so you don't think I've settled down to a normal life, we've entered an HWM Alta for the last historic Grand Prix to be held at Montlhery, a banked race circuit, just outside Paris. I've bought a red leather racing helmet and shortly I will reveal my true identity – Red Mask, my hero from 1937, kept alive purely by imagination. And a strong desire to be out when the Headless Horseman calls.

INDEX

Adam, Paul 151
Adventures of Captain Dangerfield, The 127, 131
Allen, Woody 96
'Allo 'Allo 2, 70, 150–8
Anakin, Ken 73
Angel, Danny 70
Arden, Brooks 94
Arden, Eve 55, 57, 94
Are You Being Served? 3, 122–3, 132, 137, 150–2, 158, 161
Are You Being Served Again? 151
Ashby, Carole 159
Astaire, Fred 118
Avengers, The 104–7

Bailey, F. Lee 133
Baker and Douglas 45
Bannister, Trevor 123
Beans of Boston 124, 126, 127
Belli, Marvin 133
Bennett, Harold 123, 124
Bennett, Professor 161
Berry, Rex 57–66
Betjeman, John 137
Beverly Hills Hotel 93–4, 115
Bible Explorers, The 147, 149
Billy Cotton Show 46–7, 49, 50, 58, 60, 65, 107
Blair, Joyce 45
Blair, Lionel 45, 76, 85
Boddington family 60, 64–6
Bostrom, Arthur 153
Brands Hatch 138–41
Bricusse, Evie 115–16
Bricusse, Leslie 115–16, 117–18
Bron, Eleanor 144

Bronsburg, Andy 76
Brough, Arthur 123
Burness, Felix 158
Buzzi, Ruth 113

Caine, Michael 52
Campion, Gerry 76
'Captain Beaky' 137, 138, 141–4, 146, 158–9
Carne, Judy 113
Cassani, Santos 52
Castle, Roy 45
Chaplin, Charlie 150
Chapman, Colin 47, 49
Clarke, Petula 137, 143
Clements, John 74
Clithero, Jimmy 119
Connolly, Billy 110
Connor, Kenneth 155
Cook, Peter 80
Cooper, Tommy 51
Cotton, Bill, Jr 46–7
Crazy Gang 51
Croft, Ann 3
Croft, David 2–3, 122–6, 148, 150–1, 162

Dankworth, Johnny 138
Davis, Jack 72, 119, 121
Davis, Sammy, Jr 96
Dawson, Dickie 46
Delaney, Reverend Peter 144–5
Denham Flying Club 48
Desert Island Discs 107
Dickie Henderson Show 50, 57, 71, 110
Didsbury 3–5, 13–21, 159
Dietrich, Marlene 76

Doctor in Clover 107
Dors, Diana 46
Douglas, Kirk 116
Dunwell, Doctor 5–11, 24, 70, 137, 167

Ediswan Electric Company 32–3
Edmonds, Noel 138, 140–1, 143
Elstree Studios 55
English, Arthur 123
Estartit, Costa Brava 57–66
Eve Arden Special 159

Faith, Adam 41
Fantasy Island 128, 131
Field, Shirley Ann 107, 108–9
Flynn, Errol 48, 135, 139
Forbes, Bryan 79–80
Forsythe, Bruce 45
Four Musketeers, The 159
Fowlds, Derek 68
Fox, James 70, 72–3

Garcia, Juan 61, 64–5
Georgie Girl 77
Gibson, Richard 153, 154–5
Good, Jack 42
Goodwood 49–50
Goon Show 45
Grace and Favour 123, 151, 153
Grafton Arms 45, 50, 71, 74, 77, 86, 96, 110, 151
Grafton, Major Jimmy 45–6, 49–50, 51, 71, 86, 110–11
Gray, Thomas 25

Haig, Jack 151
Hamilton, George 136
Happy Days 124, 125
Hardisty, Miss 4
Harper, Gerald 138
Hawn, Goldie 113
Hellerman, John 125
Hempel, Anouska 132
Henderson, Dickie 57, 61
Hill, Rose 154, 155–7
Hobbs, John 153
Hodge, Sue 158
Horizon Tours 63, 64

Inman, John 123, 138
It's Awfully Bad For Your Eyes, Darling! 122

Jack's Club, Orange Street 50–1
Jackson, Gordon 137, 143
Joan, Dr 146
Johnson, Artie 111, 113, 114
Johnson, Coslough 111, 114
Just For Fun! 88
Justice, James Robertson 72, 107

Kaye, Danny 36, 113, 114
Kaye, Gorden 149, 150, 152–3, 158
Keith, Penelope 143
Keyes, Paul 113
Kinks, The 76

Landen, Dinsdale 68
Lane, Lupino 12
Laugh In see Rowan and Martin
Lawford, Peter 96
Lee, Peter 71
Lees, Margo 118, 144
Leigh, Vivien 51
Leonard, Josie 52
Lloyd, Dawn 36, 48, 51–2, 55–7, 71, 74
Lloyd, Sue 104–6
Losey, Joseph 70, 73
Loss, Joe 24
Lumley, Joanna 36, 118–20, 122, 164–5

Mad Moments 115
Man in the Moon 108
Manson, Charles 116
Marner, Richard 153
Marshall, Gary 124, 125
Martin, Dick 113
Merv Griffin Show 146
Michell, Keith 74, 136, 137, 143, 144
Michelle, Vicki 153, 158
Mills Circus family 24, 52
Mills, Freddy 44
Minnelli, Liza 144
Montalban, Ricardo 128
Monte Carlo 55–6, 70
Moore, Dudley 80
Moore, Roger 52
More, Kenneth 67, 68, 108
Morecambe, Eric 71
Morley, Robert 74
Moss, Stirling 51
Mower, Patrick 132
Muir, Jean 118
Murray, Pete 42

New Look 44–6
Newmar, Julie 112, 115
Niven, David 134–6
Northrop, Collette 167

Oakie, Jackie 94
Oates, Simon 104
Oberon, Merle 36, 116
Oh, Happy Band 150
Olivier, Laurence 53
O'Mara, Kate 104–6
O'Neal, Ryan 96
O'Neil, Terry 68

Index

Parker, Jim 137, 141
Parkinson, Michael 107
Parsons, Nicholas 138
Percival, Lance 132–3
Pertwee, Jon 42, 87, 132
Phillips, Leslie 72, 104–5, 107, 159
Pidgeon, Walter 126
Pinewood Film Studios 41, 88, 107
Place Theatre, Manchester 75
Polanski, Roman 116

Rampling, Charlotte 36, 77, 81, 95–7
Reagan, Ronald 113
Redgrave family 36
Redgrave, Lynn 96
Red Mask 9, 36, 167
Reposo, Joe 147
Reynolds, Burt 113
Rhodes, Ginny 97–100
Rhodes, Penny 97–101
Richards, Angela 75–6
Richards, Wendy 123
Rigg, Diana 1
Ritz, Harry 124–5
Robbins, Harold 77–9, 81, 93–4, 110
Robert and Elizabeth 74–7, 93, 136
Robinson, Joe and Doug 50
Rowan and Martin's Laugh In 70, 94, 110–17,
    145, 158
Rowan, Dan 113
Rowlands, Jonathan 136–7
Ruislip Trading Estate 36
Rush, Herman 124, 125, 127, 131, 146,
    148–9

St John, Earl 41
School for Scoundrels 47
Secombe, Harry 45, 50, 137, 143, 159
Sellers, Peter 137, 143
Servant, The 70, 73
Shelby, Nicole 81
Shepherd, Nona 142
Silvera, Carmen 153
Sim, Alastair 47
Simpson's of Piccadilly 33–5
Siner, Guy 154

Six Five Special 42, 44
Skellern, Peter 143
Slaughter, George 110–11, 113, 116
Smashing Time 96
Smith, Nicholas 123
Smith, Shrapnel Boisey 27–9, 145
Stamp, Terence 52
Standard Range and Foundry 30
Stevens, Ronnie 45
Stoke Court 25–6, 29, 30, 117, 144
Sues, Alan 113, 125
Sugden, Molly 123

Take Him, He's Yours 55
Tate, Sharon 116
Terry-Thomas 47, 50, 72
Tessler, Brian 44
Thornton, Frank 123
*Those Magnificent Men In Their Flying
    Machines* 72–3
Tinker, Jack 144
Toluca Capri Motel 111, 112
Toye, Wendy 67, 74–5, 78
Tushingham, Rita 96
Twiggy 137, 144

Very Important Person, A 71–2, 159

Warhol, Andy 142
Warner, David 69
Weiner, Jack 134, 135
We Joined The Navy 67
Wembley 1, 22–3
What a Whopper 41
White, Whitington 48
Whodunnit? 132–3
Williams, Robin 124
Wisdom, Norman 72
Wise, Ernie 71
Wood Green Empire 45–6, 51, 71
Woodland Gospels 145, 146
Wootton, Derek 31, 35
Worth, Harry 150
Wren, Christopher 24–5, 27
Wrong Box, The 79–81
Wynn, Jo 124, 125–7